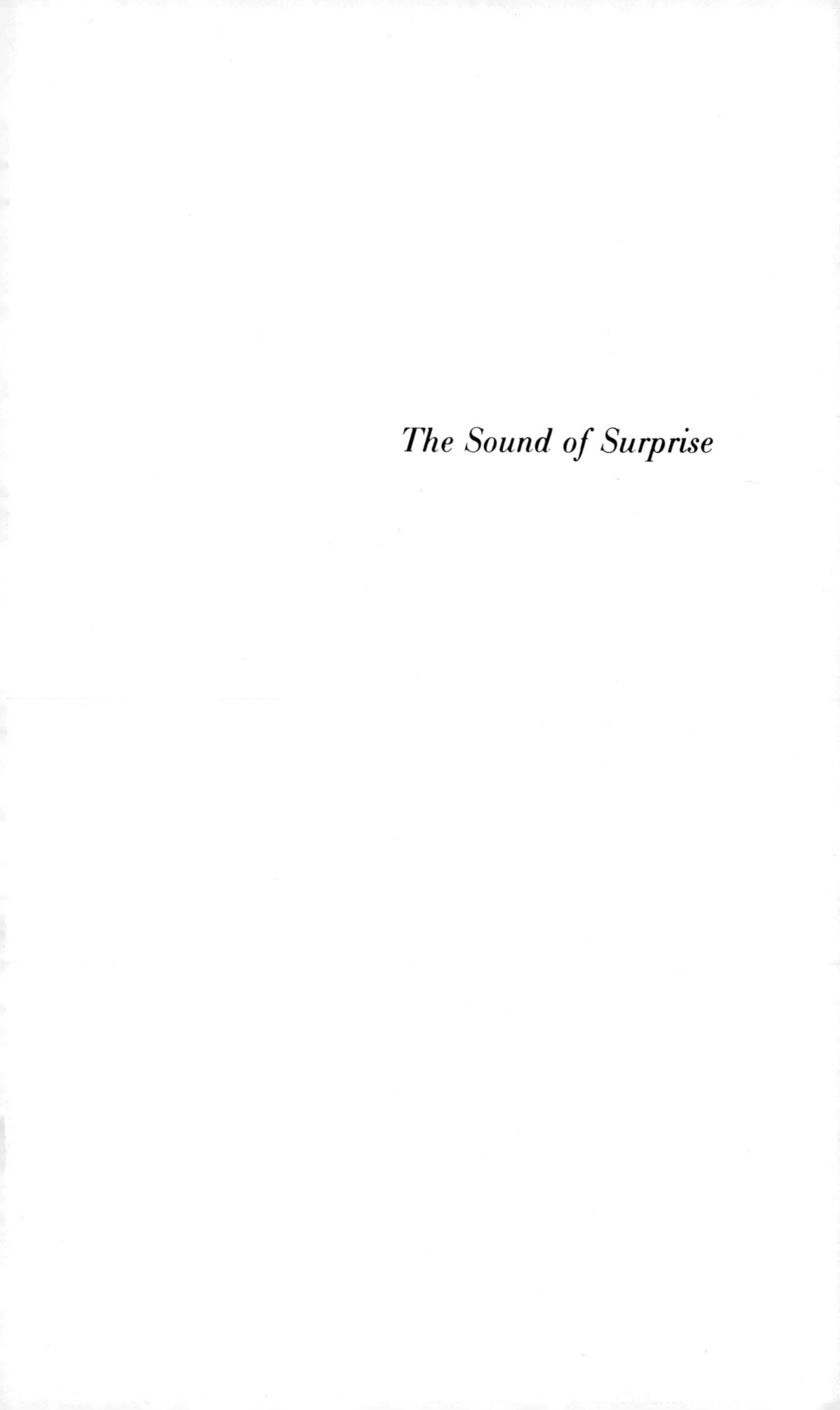

The Sound of Surprise

A Da Capo Press Reprint Series

THE ROOTS OF JAZZ

WHITNEY BALLIETT

The Sound of Surprise

46 Pieces on Jazz

DA CAPO PRESS • NEW YORK • 1978

Library of Congress Cataloging in Publication Data

Balliett, Whitney.
The sound of surprise.

(The Roots of jazz)
Reprint of the ed. published by Dutton, New York.
1. Jazz music. I. Title.
[ML3561.J3B25 1978] 785.4'2'08 77-17852
ISBN 0-306-77543-3

This Da Capo Press edition of *The Sound of Surprise*
is an unabridged republication of the paperback edition
published in New York in 1961. It is reprinted
by permission of E. P. Dutton & Co., Inc.

Published by Da Capo Press, Inc.
A Subsidiary of Plenum Publishing Corporation
227 West 17th Street, New York, N.Y. 10011

The Sound of Surprise

WHITNEY BALLIETT was born in New York City and educated at Phillips Exeter Academy. Since his graduation from Cornell University in 1951, he has been on the staff of *The New Yorker*. He is currently staff reporter, jazz columnist and critic of the off-Broadway theatre for that magazine. His poetry has appeared in *The New Yorker*, *The Atlantic* and *The Saturday Review*.

THE SOUND OF SURPRISE was first published in 1959.

WHITNEY BALLIETT

The Sound of Surprise

46 Pieces on Jazz

NEW YORK
E. P. DUTTON & CO., INC.
1961

This paperback edition of
"THE SOUND OF SURPRISE"
Published 1961 by
E. P. Dutton & Co., Inc.

FIRST EDITION

Except for the first two pieces which appeared in slightly different form in the Saturday Review *and the principal section of the third piece, which appeared, again in slightly different form, in* The Reporter, *the material in this book appeared originally in* The New Yorker *and was copyrighted in 1957, 1958 and 1959 by The New Yorker Magazine, Inc.*

LIBRARY OF CONGRESS CATALOG CARD NUMBER: 59–5832

To E. K. B.

CONTENTS

Part Three: 1958

Part Four: 1959

INTRODUCTION

It's a compliment to jazz that nine-tenths of the voluminous writing about it is bad, for the best forms often attract the most unbalanced admiration. At the same time, it is remarkable that so fragile a music has withstood such truckloads of enthusiasm. Jazz, after all, is a highly personal, lightweight form—like poetry, it is an art of surprise—that, shaken down, amounts to the blues, some unique vocal and instrumental sounds, and the limited, elusive genius of improvisation (some of it in the set forms of jazz composition). At best, these can provoke an intense, sometimes profound emotional satisfaction, which is altogether different—largely because of sheer mathematical proportions—from that induced by the design and mass of, say, Berlioz's "Requiem." The only excuse for collecting these pieces is that (the shufflings and reshufflings of taste considered) they seem to me to form a kind of selective critical documentary of the most bewildering years in the music's brief history. I also hope that such an approach, which has never been done exactly in this way before, at least breathes on some of the aesthetic mysteries of the music.

Although all the pieces have been revised, they have been kept in the order written (the dates are of publication), both for the sake of the record and to preserve a partly accidental variety of texture, pace, and subject matter. (There is one exception—a short book review, which, though written not long ago, has been put in Part One because it seemed too short to stand alone in its proper place.) It might have appeared more ambitious to rearrange the pieces, but it would also have destroyed whatever documentary aspects their present order has. Thus, these are some of the patterns—now direct, now oblique—that should emerge.

Perhaps the weightiest occurrence in jazz during recent years has been the revolution in jazz composition and arranging, which were, with the help of Jelly Roll Morton and Fletcher Henderson, practically invented by Duke Ellington. It was not until a few years ago that men like Jimmy Giuffre, Charlie Mingus, Thelonious Monk, John Lewis, George Russell, and Gil Evans began using the greater technical facilities first opened up to jazz by bebop to enlarge upon Ellington's methods. These men have also gone back to the blues, collective playing, and unashamed lyricism, all of which, for reasons made clear in the book, began to be bypassed ten or fifteen years ago. They have, of course, often overlaid the fundamental intent of jazz—to entertain and recharge the spirit with new beauties—with such superfluities as an overimmersion in classical structures, techniques, and instrumentations. But they have also often made it possible to go back to their records again and again.

Concurrently, a brilliant crop of soloists—Cecil Taylor, Sonny Rollins, the renascent Monk, Miles Davis—have appeared, and seemingly in a matter of minutes have changed the whole design of improvisation by experimenting with such diverse approaches as highly elastic chordal frameworks upon which to improvise; themes, rather than chords, as improvisatory bases; or various rhythmic possibilities that, almost for the first time, makes rhythm as important as melody and harmony. (The one still insurmountable problem in jazz is the constant demand for freshness. Since the music hinges on improvisation, a soloist must continually produce new statements. This, in turn, makes demands that are so immediate and unflagging—more so than in any other art form—that the soloist is, often as not, forced to fall back on clichés by sheer creative exhaustion.)

But, strangely enough, these new approaches to composition and improvisation often have little to do with each other. At present, composers like Russell and Lewis tend to employ soloists in their works as a kind of solemn comic relief, while soloists like Rollins and Taylor work by themselves as much as the great solo pianists of the twenties and thirties. Someday, one hopes, these composers will begin drawing men like Rollins and Taylor *into* their works, as still free extensions of the composer.

Still another notable movement in recent years has been the gradual return, in esteem, of a good many of the great swing musicians. One can find new records again by Ben Webster, Coleman Hawkins, Jo Jones, Vic Dickenson, Teddy Wilson, and Roy Eldridge, who, by playing as well or better than they were fifteen years back, counter so well the ridiculous fashion of condemning a phase of an art simply because it is no longer new. They have also strengthened the music all around them by reaffirming its hot and eloquent origins.

Finally, there is the LP record, which has already been taken for granted, but without which most of what has just been mentioned could not have taken place; by destroying the arbitrary time limitations of 78-r.p.m. recordings it has suddenly encouraged any number of new musical approaches simply by making the room for them.

Beyond that, most of the happenings in the music since

1950 or so seem to me negative ones. Louis Armstrong, one of the first jazz musicians to become a household name, has made a spectacle of himself around the world, though he is still capable of playing and singing honestly and beautifully. The various modern schools, such as the cool, West Coast, hard bop, have frequently indicated imitative fashions rather than real musical changes, and have left no taste at all, or, in the case of hard bop, an unpleasantly angry one that has more to do with matters other than music. Men like Dickie Wells, J. C. Higginbotham, Buster Bailey, and Earl Hines are, sadly, in relatively prominent decline, while such first-rate musicians as Doc Cheatham, Emmet Berry, Joe Thomas, Lucky Thompson, Don Byas, and Bill Coleman are in obscurity, either because of expatriation or public neglect. The New Orleans revivalist movement (Turk Murphy, Wilbur de Paris, and the like), which depends on the long-cold emotions of other men (there is nothing deader than an old emotion), still flourishes. Lastly, there are two production problems that have cropped up in recent years. There are simply too many jazz records made. This has, of course, been an economic and educational advantage for the young musician, who no longer has the big bands to support him while he irons out his adolescence. It has, however, also caused a terrible lowering of standards; for the first time in jazz, businessmen are attempting to feed on what they envision as the tastes of a large, solvent audience. And second, there is the recent rash of concerts, festivals, and jazz television programs. They are, I suppose, worthwhile as spreaders of the gospel. Yet, because of their sideshow methods of presentation, they frequently spread, in a rather sinister fashion, no more than a parody of jazz. Indeed, the fundamental problem of where and how and when jazz should be displayed has become, since the music ceased being a dance form, extremely acute.

I have tried to avoid repeatedly identifying who plays what instrument by making such identifications the first time a musician is mentioned, and not again, except for lesser known men. The book is by no means comprehensive, since I simply haven't yet gotten around to a good many musicians who are just as important as those appearing here.

I should like to express gratitude to Irving Kolodin, of the *Saturday Review*, who, several years ago, taught me an incalculable amount by courageously printing my impulses about the music, and to William Shawn and Rogers Whitaker, of *The New Yorker*, whose understanding and skill have my boundless admiration.

W. B.

The Sound of Surprise

PART ONE

1954-1956

PANDEMONIUM PAYS OFF

Norman Granz, a lean, fast-talking, sandy-haired man of thirty-six, with bullying eyebrows, sends out single-handedly over a good part of the Western world a yearly series of jazz concert tours known as "Jazz at the Philharmonic," owns and operates a record company that has mushroomed so violently in its first year that it has had to be split into two companies to accommodate overworked distribution facilities and, as a canny granitic businessman, is generally regarded as the first person who has ever been able to successfully mass-produce jazz. The total worth of these enterprises is estimated by Granz at five million dollars. Of this, a million accrues from JATP, and the rest from his record firm. These staggering sums—staggering for jazz, since it was not long ago that jazzmen were dying of malnutrition and exposure—are easily accounted for, if not easily explained. Last year JATP included eleven jazz musicians and a singer, who played in fifty American and Canadian cities where seventy-five concerts were held; in Japan where twenty-four concerts were given; in Honolulu; and in twenty-five cities in Europe, where some fifty concerts occurred. The group appeared before approximately four hundred thousand persons, who paid from $2 to $4.80 for their seats. Granz's recording activities, which are sandwiched in between tours and business trips abroad, were equally cornucopic. Over two hundred ten- and twelve-inch jazz LP albums were released on the Clef and Norgran labels, and in a recent month twenty-one new Granz records flowed into record stores across the country. Columbia and Victor, who are again marketing jazz in a big way, released about forty albums apiece. In fact, perhaps 50 per cent of all the jazz records produced last year came from Granz factories, a development that has become somewhat of an uneasy joke in the industry. Granz's recording efforts are also encyclopedic. At present his catalogue lists seven LPs devoted to the work of Lester Young. Art Tatum is represented by five twelve-inch LPs, with seven more promised. Charlie Parker has eight. Johnny Hodges has five. And Oscar Peterson, the twenty-nine-year-old Canadian pianist, who has virtually been handmaidened into fame by Granz and has since become the Granz house pianist, now has sixteen titles to his credit.

Granz was born in Los Angeles, and attended UCLA, where, as a part-time quotation clerk with the Los Angeles Stock Exchange, he picked up some useful rudiments about money. After college and a stint in the Army, which was followed by a film editor's job at M-G-M, Granz, who was a jazz fan and a strong liberal, decided that jazz should be listened to in the pleasantest possible surroundings by the largest possible number of people of all races, creeds, and colors. The non-segregational concert hall was the answer. Late in 1945, after running a series of successful informal concerts at the Los Angeles Philharmonic Auditorium, he took a hand-picked group of musicians on a limited tour of the western United States and Canada.

Unfortunately, the public, unlike Barkis, was not willing, and the tour collapsed in Canada after working its way up the West Coast. A few years later, with the assistance of names on the Granz payroll like Gene Krupa, Coleman Hawkins, Bill Harris, Flip Phillips, and Buddy Rich, and with the release of the first of fifteen on-the-spot recordings of JATP concerts, the public changed its mind. In the meantime, Granz had not forgotten his liberal instincts. He succeeded in taking his groups, which have been a consistent mixture of Negro and white, into those parts of the country where racial bias still persists, and two years ago had a rider put in certain of his contracts with theater owners to the effect that if any discrimination is practiced against his audiences, the concert may immediately be canceled.

Since the shaky days of 1945 Granz's acquaintances have been continually astonished by his drive and durability in a notoriously unsympathetic business. He works without any regular assistants, outside of a few harassed secretaries and a publicity agent. Granz books almost all his own concerts, an accomplishment that was of some proportions in the pioneering days and that has since been partially alleviated by arranging future concerts in a city while his men are playing it. In line with his recent efforts to give his enterprises a single, well-honed edge, Granz now schedules concerts in new cities on the strength of his record sales in that area; for the roster of his recording artists, which numbers over a hundred, is a fairly accurate mirror, past and present, of the personnel he has had in his various JATP groups.

Granz attends every concert JATP gives, acting as both M.C. and stage manager. Out front, he seems an almost timid figure, for he is distinguished in neither voice nor presence. Backstage, however, Granz is highly inflammable. "I go crazy at concerts," he said recently. "I lose my temper every five minutes. I yell at everybody. I'm rude to people who pester me. Every concert has to go perfectly. If somebody goofs, he pays for it." But if Granz is touchy under pressure he is generally of temperate mien. Most of his musicians like working for him, and return to JATP year after year. There are occasional familial eruptions, of course, such as a falling out about a year ago that Granz had with Buddy Rich, the drummer. Rich blatantly announced in the pages of *Down Beat* magazine that he was through with JATP because Granz made his musicians play nothing but "junk." Granz answered hotly that he never told his musicians what to play, and that Rich was a "liar" and an "adolescent." A short time later Rich was contentedly thumping away on a new Granz recording date, and appeared, as usual, in last year's JATP lineup.

Granz the businessman has occasionally made profitable room for Granz the jazz lover. In 1944, for instance, he supervised one of the few honest motion pictures ever made about jazz. A short, photographed in color by Gjon Mili, and called *Jammin' the Blues*, it won an Academy Award nomination for the best short feature of the year. (Many of the musicians involved were drawn from the Granz-sponsored concert group then appearing in Los Angeles.) In 1949, when he was using the facilities of the Mercury record company, he issued a deluxe twelve-inch 78 rpm album which featured such oddities as Harry Carney, the baritone saxophone player, pitted against strings, the unorthodox arrangements of George Handy and Ralph Burns, an unaccompanied saxophone solo by Coleman Hawkins, and generous quantities of Bud Powell and Charlie Parker. The album had, in addition, a folio of handsome life-size photographs, and the whole package, five thousand of which were printed, was priced at a cool twenty-five dollars. It was sold out in a year.

Granz was the first person to experiment widely with on-the-spot recordings, and with studio recordings that took advantage of the longer playing time of the LP. Record stores have been reordering them ever since. Two years ago he released four twelve-inch LPs, titled "The Astaire Story," which showed off Fred Astaire's singing and dancing before a small Granz-picked jazz unit. The set was widely panned by the critics, but has been just as widely accepted by the public, which tends to ignore critics, a fact that Granz is well aware of.

Granz the businessman, who has become increasingly dominant in recent years, is most aggressive when he is near the concert stage. Here he believes that a small group, working within a loose framework, is the surest means of producing satisfying, free-wheeling jazz. He chooses musicians who, he feels, are the best or the near best on their instruments regardless of school or style. This does not mean that Granz would be apt to hire an excellent but largely unknown musician, for he is never unconscious of the drawing power of a name. (If Granz decides, though, that a certain unknown musician should become a member of a future JATP tour, he carefully builds his name during the preceding year by releasing several of his LPs. The most recent example of this technique has been his promotion of Buddy de Franco, the clarinettist, and Louis

Bellson, the drummer, both of whom will join JATP for the first time this year.)

The result of these policies is a nervous jazz that is somewhere between small-band swing and bebop. It is also a purely solo jazz, where collective improvisation or teamwork is left to other, more pedestrian schools. This concentration on the solo has brought off some weird musical achievements. One is a regularly featured trumpet battle—Roy Eldridge and his old pupil Dizzy Gillespie will be the participants this year—in which two trumpeters squeal at each other for chorus after chorus like stuck pigs. Another is a blinding, deafening drum battle that invariably jellies the stoutest audience. Most of the musical materials employed are banal, being restricted to the commonest type of blues, and to such evergreens as "How High the Moon" and a handful of Gershwin tunes.

Granz feels that the average age level of his audiences has increased in the past nine years, and that it is now somewhere between twenty-one and twenty-eight, a rather casual statistic, judging by the oceans of heated teenage faces found at any Granz concert. One might at first describe these audiences as the spiritual offspring of the sprites who jitterbugged in the aisles and on the stage of the Paramount Theatre in New York in the late thirties when Benny Goodman first came to town. But at second glance these present-day audiences are different, and more warlike. They rarely move from their seats, yet they manage to give off through a series of screams (the word "go" repeated like the successive slams of the cars on a fast freight), blood-stopping whistles, and stamping feet a mass intensity that would have soothed Hitler, and made Benny Goodman pale.

Granz the jazz lover is predominantly visible through his studio recording sessions. In these he has been responsible for a certain amount of excellent jazz, as well as a great deal of mediocrity. Granz officiates at every recording date, and ominously announces this fact on his record labels and sleeves with, respectively, the words "Recorded Under the Personal Supervision of Norman Granz" and "Supervised by Norman Granz." He also composes many of the liner notes for his albums, which have become noted for their superlatives and lack of information. Although Granz claims that he never dictates to his musicians, much of what emanates from his recording studios has come to have a distinct flavor. For, in spite of the fact that his personnels are often laundry lists of jazz royalty, many Granz records are luxurious wastes. One reason for this is that many of the musicians on Granz recordings are members of JATP, and, because of the nature of the music they play seven months out of the year on the concert stage, their musical batteries have gone dead. And if a touring job with Granz often makes his musicians artistically laconic, it has also not advanced the musical growth of such men as Flip Phillips, Oscar Peterson, Charlie Shavers, and Buddy Rich.

When Granz inaugurated this year's JATP tour on September 17, in Hartford, he had eleven of the best jazz musicians money can buy. He is paying them salaries that start at several hundred dollars a week, and range up to $6,000 a week for Ella Fitzgerald and $5,000 for Peterson. In addition to the European tour in the spring, and the fall tour of the United States and Canada, JATP will swing through Australia, as well as Japan and Honolulu. Granz has also promised a minimum of 120 LP albums in the next twelve months. To at least half a million potential customers around the world Granz may well be doing for jazz what another prestidigitator, P. T. Barnum, did for midgets.

September 25, 1954

ARTISTRY IN LIMBO

Stan Kenton got started officially as a band leader on Memorial Day, 1940, when he opened with a thirteen-piece group at the Rendezvous Ballroom in Balboa, California. The music, already indicative of things to come, was relentless and heavy-booted, with a staccato two-beat attack that resembled in intent, if not execution, the style of the Lunceford band of the time. Perhaps it was persuasive because it was rhythmically overpowering, for by the summer's end, Kenton had built a staunch following on the West Coast and considerable speculation about his "new music" in the East. Kenton's second period began in 1944 after he had been East, and, although the band was defter and less aggressive, it was not much different. The third era, 1945–46, illustrated what is now known as the band's principal style—a big reed section securely rooted with a baritone saxophone, an inflexible, metallic-sounding rhythm section, and ear-bursting brass teams. The next two periods extended from 1947 to 1951, years in which Kenton turned restlessly to his "progressive jazz" and "innovations in modern music," using, in addition to his own works, the compositions and arrangements of Bob Graettinger, Pete Rugulo, Ken Hanna, Neil Hefti, and Shorty Rogers. Here the music moved ceaselessly and cumbersomely between the funereal orchestrations of Graettinger, mood music performed by a forty-piece band with strings that was perilously close to movie music, and immense jazzlike frameworks constructed about scintillating section work and occasional soloists. The last era, which brings the band up through 1953, was more or less of a deflation to the mid-forties period, and reveals a clearer jazz feeling than the band had ever before had.

It is impossible not to be impressed by Kenton's aural bulk, by the sheer sinew and muscle that have gone into his music. It is not impossible, however, to remain almost completely unmoved. Kenton's bands, in spite of all the complacent, organlike talk that has surrounded their "progressivism" in the past ten years, fit roughly into the tradition of the silvery semi-jazz groups of Larry Clinton, Glen Gray, Glenn Miller, the Dorseys, and Ray Anthony. This tradition, although aereated from time to time by Bunny Berigans and Bobby Hacketts, is quite different from the genuine big jazz bands cradled by Fletcher Henderson and Duke Ellington, and maintained since by Goodman, Lunceford, Calloway, Basie, and Woody Herman. Kenton does not fit easily into the white-collar music of the former tradition, however, for he tried to combine the two movements, with the help of extracurricular seasonings, into something new. This he did, in part, by allowing ample solo space within glistening limousines of sound that, in the end, tended only to stifle whatever potentialities for jazz there were on hand. He also created, as a result of purposely and confusedly trying to be a musical refractor of his times, a self-conscious music that was caught—strident and humorless—somewhere between the pseudo-classical, jazz, and popular music.

Nevertheless, Kenton's sounds and furies have, partly

through accident, had certain positive effects within jazz. His various bands have been rigorous training grounds for many younger musicians, particularly those who have gone on to fashion in the past few years, in probable revolt, the small-band parlor jazz of the West Coast. His pelting about of words like "progressive" and "innovation," together with the uncompromisingly modernistic tenor of his music, has helped prepare the public for true futurists like Gillespie, Parker, Monk, Powell, and John Lewis. And, finally, he has inadvertently defined, like a Thomas Wolfe, the possible wastelands of his own medium, thus performing the negative service of showing many jazzmen where not to tread.

Kenton says in the epilogue to a recent album called "The Kenton Era" that "It is too early yet to attempt to ascertain whether our efforts over the years have contributed to the development of the world's music." It isn't, of course, for—as is apparent in this album—his music has come just about full circle. Indeed, it deserves a prominent place in that fascinating museum where the curiosities of music are stored.

April 30, 1955

THE BIBULOUS AUNT

It has become customary, during the thirty-five or so years in which a body of critical writing has sprung up around jazz, for its authors to preface their remarks with indignant statements about all the "nonsense" written on the subject, and then sit down and write some more. There are, of course, good reasons for this. Until the past five or so years, jazz has been widely regarded in this country as a kind of queer Victorian aunt who laces her tea, belches at the wrong moment, and uses improper amounts of rouge. As a result, its defenders or, better, apologists have often been guilty of a harmful immoderation—hot, gassy prose, provincialism, inaccuracy, and condescension—originally born, like the intentions of the back-seat driver, of a fervent desire to help. But now jazz is played in concert halls and colleges around the world, as well as taught in accredited university courses. It is sent abroad under the sponsorship of the U. S. State Department as a benevolent cultural ambassador. Heavily attended summer festivals of jazz are sprouting around the country. The New York *Times* has a jazz critic. And lastly, jazz has become, with the combined help of the long-playing record and an economic boom, a big business—perhaps the most heartfelt blessing Americans can bestow on a native endeavor.

Europeans have loved, if not always understood, jazz

almost since its inception. In 1919, Ernest Ansermet, the Swiss conductor, wrote with perception about Sidney Bechet, whom he had heard in London. A few years later, a German published a short book with the engaging title *Jazz und Shimmy,* which was followed by *Das Jazz-Buch.* (There is something about the German language that is all elbows and belly when it comes to jazz; in the 1930's, another German wrote a paper called "Was Ist mit der Jazzmusik?") Then in 1932 Robert Goffin, a Belgian, wrote what amounts to the first real book about jazz. In the meantime, American magazines like the *Ladies' Home Journal, Literary Digest,* and *Etude* were boiling over with pieces called "Is Jazz the Pilot of Disaster?", "The Doctor Looks at Jazz," "Unspeakable Jazz Must Go!," and "Does Jazz Put the Sin in Syncopation?" And in 1926 a man named Henry O. Osgood wrote a solemn, seemingly official book, *So This Is Jazz,* which didn't mention a single jazz musician, but pored reverently over the works of "jazz" composers like Gershwin and Ferde Grofé. In fact, it was not until 1938, when Winthrop Sargeant and Wilder Hobson produced their still valuable books, *Jazz: Hot and Hybrid* and *American Jazz Music,* that the first full-dress American analytical works were written on the subject. Since then, books on jazz by Americans have been piling up on remainder counters like politicians' diaries, and in some sort of mid-century ecstasy there have recently appeared a discography of LP records, a couple of histories, several autobiographies, a biography, an encyclopedia, and two bibliographies, one of which has well over three thousand entries.

Possibly because zealots have a weakness for the convenient half of any truth, many books on jazz have been highly personalized histories, full of myth, sentimentality, and blowzy writing. *The Real Jazz Old and New* (Louisiana University State Press), by Stephen Longstreet, is no exception. The author, who is perhaps best known as a screen writer, has compiled, in the form of a history, a great many supposed quotes taken down from nameless jazz musicians, and has packed them in between a whimsy of his own. He explains, for example, that Buddy Bolden, the legendary New Orleans cornetist, was committed to a state institution for the insane in 1907 (he was), and then declares later on that Bolden "may have made the first jazz recordings around 1912." (It has been fairly well proved that Bolden did record, but it was probably around the turn of the century; if the cylinders are ever found, they'll be roughly equivalent in worth to the Rosetta stone.) Charlie "Big" Green, a trombonist, who is supposed to have frozen to death one night on a Harlem doorstep, becomes Charlie Long Green. The first bebop recordings, made in 1944 under Coleman Hawkins' name, are reported to have been released on the "Bluebird" label, instead of the Apollo label. And in his introduction Mr. Longstreet says, "I don't know of another book like [mine]—that lets the jazzmen tell their own story in their own words." Such a book was published well over a year ago—*Hear Me Talkin' to Ya*, edited by Nat Shapiro and Nat Hentoff (Rinehart).

Hugues Panassié, a blindingly prejudiced but goodhearted French critic who published one of the pioneering books on jazz, *Le Jazz Hot*, in 1934, and who, through some mysterious chemistry, was chosen to write the entry on jazz for the recently issued fifth edition of *Grove's Dictionary of Music and Musicians*, is far guiltier of unscrupulously uncinching his ego than Longstreet, who at least makes no pretense at being more than an amateur. For Panassié's new book, *Guide to Jazz* (Houghton Mifflin), done with Madeleine Gautier, which Louis Armstrong describes in a short preface as "the musicians' Bible" (Panassié later retaliates by calling Armstrong "a genius comparable with the greatest names in the history of music"), is a collection of opinions, peppered with facts, on jazz musicians, songs, jazz categories, and musical terms. It is also very entertaining reading, for Panassié is a jubilantly wrongheaded critic who champions his unwillingness to understand all jazz produced since 1940. Thus, bebop is a disease, and any musician who has become contaminated is either unmentionable or is straight-armed, like the late Charlie Parker: "An extremely gifted musician, Parker gradually gave up jazz in favor of bop . . ." Panassié's book does, however, provide a distinct, if sometimes abortive, service by listing dozens of the now obscure or dead rural and urban blues musicians and singers. The fact that some of these entries are all but useless (JENKINS, MYRTLE Piano. Very good in blues, and has made a number of records accompanying blues singers, notably: with Bumble Bee Slim, "New Bricks in My Pillow," "When I Get My Money," 1936), is, of course, partly due to a genuine dearth of information on the subject, as well as, one suspects, to the casualness that elsewhere leads Panassié to label Snooky Young, the trumpeter, as a trombonist.

The Heart of Jazz (New York University Press), by William L. Grossman (an associate professor at the New York University School of Commerce) and Jack W. Farrell (a jazz collector), is similar—at least so far as good, raw prejudice is concerned—to the efforts of Longstreet and Panassié. Written in a bearded drone punctuated with footnotes and phrases like "the nonsensicality of content" (inherent in the trumpet playing of Dizzy Gillespie), the book is by far the canniest and most subtle defense of the moldy-fig school of jazz appreciation that we have yet had.

Grossman puts his shoulder to the moldy-fig dogma with tortoise-like deliberation. Gradually he builds a fustian image of the old New Orleans musician as a carefree, humble, and saintly Uncle Tom who somehow crystallized in his music both the reason and freedom of the humanist and the selfless dignity of the Christian. (Grossman plants this theory squarely on the supposition that the "contents" of any music can be unalterably fixed, like the price of pork.) Then, he says, along came Louis Armstrong and in 1925 began destroying the religious content in New Orleans jazz through an act of "apostasy," by becoming a self-serving soloist rather than an integrated part of the traditional New Orleans ensemble structure, which has few if any solos. Grossman heaps most of the evils he finds in swing, bebop, and progressive jazz on poor Armstrong, describing him as playing with "an expertly controlled barbaric yawp," "frenzy," "an undisciplined emotional expansiveness," and "wildness." (A contemporary of Armstrong's, Jabbo Smith, who fits these phrases to a "T," is not mentioned in the book.) The remedy for this unfortunate heresy, Grossman eventually tells us, is that jazz musicians must rediscover the original "Judeo-Christian content" of New Orleans jazz—the origins of which, of course, are now as remote as Chellean man simply because the environment in New Orleans sixty and more years ago will never again exist.

Fortunately, neither André Hodeir, in his *Jazz: Its Evolution and Essence* (Grove Press), nor Marshall Stearns in *The Story of Jazz* (Oxford University Press) has to labor along under this blarney advanced by Grossman early in his argument: "It would indeed be curious if, upon careful critical examination, two very different directions in a creative art were found equally desirable." Hodeir, a cool-minded young French composer and critic, has written a rather dry and difficult semi-musicological study of jazz that seeks—and often finds—profound insights into the methods of musicians, ranging from the New Orleans clarinettist Johnny Dodds to Charlie Parker. (Dodds is unstintingly praised by Messrs. Grossman and Farrell and is both praised and sharply criticized by Hodeir for his obvious musical sloppiness.) If the book has a fault, it is a hyper-intensity that leads Mr. Hodeir into the hushed zones of French theoretical criticism, where, in prying into the very "essence" of jazz, he bravely strips it of its two fundamentals, improvisation and the blues.

Stearns is an associate professor of medieval history at Hunter College, and his book is a smooth and often witty attempt to trace jazz from the cultures current in West Africa two hundred years ago to the enormously complicated mixture it has become. He has been criticized for having produced a disappointingly incomplete history of jazz, but it seems fairly certain that he had little intention of writing such a work, which would at the time be premature and even impossible. What he has done, however, is give a broad indication, largely gathered from the research of social scientists, as to where many of the religious and secular sources that went into jazz—the English hymn, the spiritual, the blues, African rhythms, the

French quadrille, European band music, and the like—came from and how they reacted on one another. There is also, among other things, a sensitive chapter on the tricky attitudes of the Negro toward the white and vice versa, as well as a rather confusing section, in which he tries, with a kind of cinematic transition technique, to map out what was happening simultaneously in jazz in the 1920's and 1930's from Florida to Oregon. At any rate, Stearns is indicating, along with Hodeir, that the bibulous aunt has been reformed.

December 27, 1956

One of the smaller but more durable mysteries of the past twenty years has been the almost total lack of success that novelists and short-story writers have had in dealing with jazz. Jazz is notably unsentimental, as are, in the main, the people who play it. Yet countless drooping, bleary novels and stories have appeared in which jazz musicians, postured in various awkward attitudes, like bad statuary, produce a homely, cathartic, semi-divine music. At the same time, jazz seems to provide a safety valve for these writers, who invariably let loose a thick, sticky spray of metaphor and simile that forms a bad counterpoint to the subject matter. Here is a paragraph from *The Horn* (Random House), a new novel about a saxophonist named Edgar Pool, by John Clellon Holmes, one of the pioneer chroniclers of the world Jack Kerouac presides over:

> [Pool] fled down the immemorial Big River of his music, wanting to follow moving water because it went somewhere, and all complexities and attitudes and wraths

were swept away before it. And so he fled down the Great Brown Snake that made the entire continent one vast watershed to it, and that from deepest, woodsy north at its trickling beginnings over smooth Canadian pebbles, to its final, timeless spending in the Gulf, drained out of the heart of America, melling Pittsburgh slag from the Monongahela with dust that blew across the faceless Badlands to the Milk . . . until in huge, instinctive death beyond the last bayous, it joined the other waters of the world.

In the rare moments when Mr. Holmes pauses for breath, he tells with considerable authenticity of the last twenty-four hours in the life of Pool, who suggests a combination of the tenor saxophonist Lester Young and the late alto saxophonist Charlie Parker (incidents in Pool's life seem to be lifted directly from well-known events or legends in Young's and Parker's careers). But then the rhapsody shuts down again, and after a couple of hundred pages one's sense of pity for, or even understanding of, Pool's misery is hopelessly dampened. Mr. Holmes says, in a note, that his book, "like the music that it celebrates, is a collective improvisation on an American theme; and if there are truths here, they are poetic truths." What Mr. Holmes probably means—if he means anything—is poetical truths. There are plenty of those.

September 6, 1958

PART TWO

1957

PROGRESS AND PRUDENCE

TRANSITION, a small and apparently fearless firm in Cambridge, Massachusetts, has issued a brilliant, uncompromising record on which the principal performer is a twenty-three-year-old pianist named Cecil Taylor. "Jazz Advance: The Cecil Taylor Quartet," the record in question, offers two possibilities. It could have the same revolutionary impact upon modern jazz as the recordings of Charlie Parker, or, because it rejects both the listener and standard jazz procedure with an almost vindictive vigor, it could go the ineffectual way of the peculiarly defiant big-brass-band works of Stan Kenton. Taylor is a graduate of the New England Conservatory of Music, and his technique and knowledge of music are, like those of most young jazz pianists, more than adequate. But, unlike many of his colleagues, he has a musical imagination that is, within its chosen limits, astonishing. In the six selections on the disc (one apiece by Thelonious Monk, Duke Ellington, and Cole Porter, and the rest by Taylor), he plunges—usually backed by two or three sidemen—into a type of daring jazz improvisation that has been tried occasionally by men like Sonny Rollins, Lennie Tristano, and Charlie Mingus. Heretofore, a classic jazz solo has often been regarded as the creation, from a melody or a set of chords, of a heightened alter-melody that can, in the hands of such a master as Coleman Hawkins, be a far more compelling composition than the original. Taylor goes one step further; in, for example, "Charge 'Em Blues" and "Azure" he replaces all the original melodic content with a seemingly disconnected series of hard, jagged, and at times even ugly atonal structures that are jerked back and forth by rhythmic patterns that shift with bewildering speed and frequency. It is exhausting music; in addition to its demanding harmonic and rhythmic complexities, it has considerable power and emotion. Taylor batters us one second with moody, Monklike dissonances, the next second with a nervous legato run that would be Debussyan were it not so slyly stated, and then with a rush of grinding, staccato chords. This is followed by a short, jolting pause before he goes galloping off again. Yet despite all this strutting activity, each number sounds pretty much like the others. For there is an overweening muddiness that is due in part to the density of Taylor's style and in part to his habit of mixing in bits and pieces of, apparently, every one of the musical traditions he has ever been in contact with. Under the circumstances, Taylor's drummer, Dennis Charles, and his bass player, Buell Neidlinger, are remarkable. Charles, a fairly thunderous worker, is uncanny at divining just in time which tortuous rhythmic path his leader is about to explore. The addition, in two numbers, of the keening, lemony soprano saxophone of Steve Lacy is, in the face of the fireworks it must contend with, rather unfortunate.

Although Gerry Mulligan, composer, arranger, and baritone saxophonist, has never shied at the experimental, his new record, "Mainstream of Jazz" (EmArcy), sounds, after Taylor's awesome effusions, like a Louis Armstrong Hot Five. But if Mulligan is more cautious than Taylor, he is also on firmer ground. Taylor stuns us with the curious; Mulligan beguiles us by refining the accepted with unflagging warmth and intelligence. In fact, the sextet he employs for this record—Jon Eardley or Don Ferrara, trumpet; Zoot Sims, tenor saxophone; Bobby Brookmeyer, valve trombone; Bill Crow, bass; and Dave Bailey, drums—becomes a self-charging unit that can be traced directly to Jelly Roll Morton's Red Hot Peppers and the early Duke Ellington. There are six numbers, three of them written by Mulligan, and in every one he uses the devices that worked so well with his pioneer quartet (trumpet, baritone saxophone, bass, and drums) of several years ago—casual, baggy counterpoint, subtle dynamics, sensitive exploration of instrumental timbres, and again the absence of a piano (except in "Blue at the Roots," for which Mulligan sits down at the keyboard, with original results). For example, Mulligan inserts, usually after the solos, patches of loose yet thickly textured counterpoint, in which all or some of the melody instruments noodle around for several choruses at a time with contrasting figures—in "Igloo" with a plaintive humming effect, in "Elevation" with an irresistible butting intensity. This refreshing polyphony spills over into the solos, which are often framed by softly stated chords of counter-melodies that throw the soloist into even bolder relief, while discreetly reminding him that he is still part of a group. The result is a relaxed, intricate busyness that is a pleasing contrast to the widespread practice among modern jazz musicians of allowing soloist after soloist to perform at excessive—

and generally vacuous—length, supported by an inevitably metronomic rhythm section. All the Mulligan musicians are in top form. Sims' bushy tone (particularly in a long and engaging duet with Mulligan in "Mainstream") has never been more effectively recorded, nor has Brookmeyer's inventive and impeccable trombone.

April 13

THE DUKE AT PLAY

Duke Ellington, the ingenious composer, arranger, and band leader, is reportedly staging a comeback—the mysterious, often imaginary trek that almost every American artist who has a press agent worth his salt makes at least once in his career. Ellington, whose music continues to color nearly every corner of jazz, and whose songs and serious works rank with any produced in this country, has, of course, been suffering not from oblivion but from a combination of personnel problems within his band and the generally watery economic condition of the big-band business. In its resurgence, his outfit is playing with more punch and persuasiveness than it has in a decade, and Ellington himself, who has always used his orchestra as a proving ground for his compositions, has begun to write large, ambitious pieces again. In the past year or so—in addition to bringing the Newport Jazz Festival to a memorably ringing climax—he has composed and performed a suite based on Shakespeare's plays, and has concocted a musical and dramatic fantasy, *A Drum Is a Woman,* which was presented Wednesday night last week as an hour-long show on C.B.S. television. The show marked the first time that a full-length musical-dramatic creation written by Ellington (and Billy Strayhorn, his musical right hand) had been presented anywhere, but, aside from its inspired title, it was an almost embarrassingly flimsy affair, which failed both as a piece of light nonsense and as a true indication of Ellington's abilities.

The work was adapted for television, with only minor changes, from a recently recorded version, and is, loosely, a symbolic, tongue-in-cheek retelling of the history of jazz. It revolves around two figures—Carribee Joe, a jungle drummer, who represents the African origins of jazz, and Madam Zajj, who is the music that has evolved. Madam Zajj, at first a drum, metamorphoses into a flashy, snaky woman, who travels by hurtling through the sky on the trade winds or by driving an eighty-eight-cylinder car at four hundred and forty miles an hour. She and Carribee Joe sing and dance heatedly to express their love for one another, in a series of episodes, introduced and commented on by Ellington, that are set in Barbados, in New Orleans, at Mardi Gras time, in a Chicago night club, in a Fifty-second Street night club, and on a spot near the moon. The rest of the work, for the purposes of television, was filled, rather desperately, by an extraordinary amount of sinewy, perspiring modern ballet, which was choreographed by Paul Godkin and executed, with a lot more gesture than meaning, by a sizable group. Margaret Tynes, a dramatic soprano, and Joya Sherrill, a singer who has worked with Ellington in the past, shared the role of Madam Zajj (she was danced by Carmen de Lavallade) and sang it with ease and clarity, and Carribee Joe (danced by Talley Beatty) was handled more than adequately by Ozzie Bailey. Unfortunately, the Ellington band was seen and heard only fitfully, but there were brief, spirited solo passages by nearly everyone, including Clark Terry and Ray Nance, trumpets; Russell Procope, clarinet; Johnny Hodges, alto saxophone; and Sam Woodyard, drums. The music, which consisted of thirteen numbers, some of them instrumentals, seemed incidental at times. It ranged from a calypso ("What Else Can You Do with a Drum?"), which had a good deal of melodic charm, to a couple of dramatic, almost operatic laments (the title song and "Carribee Joe"). Ellington appeared half a dozen times or so, resplendent in white tie and tails, and delivered such Technicolor periods as "The Mississippi River, a puddle of Pekin blue pudding, pistachio and indigo" and "His heartbeat was like bongos" with so much conviction and charm that they seemed almost possible.

On Saturday evening, a new big band, led by Johnny Richards, gave a concert, along with the Horace Silver Quintet, at Town Hall, and it may well have been the most stentorian event of its kind ever held. Richards' group, which played for roughly two-thirds of the time, was a seventeen-piece organization that demonstrated much of the polish and all of the alarming, froglike volume of Stan Kenton. (Richards has worked for Kenton as an arranger and composer off and on for the past ten years.) In addition to piano, bass, and drums, its brassy, basso-profundo instrumentation included four trumpets, three trombones, a French horn, a tuba, a bass saxophone, a baritone saxophone, timpani, and an alto and a tenor saxophone. All but two of the dozen-odd pieces heard were by Richards. Top-heavy structures, full of tight, convoluted scoring that was frequently punctuated or underlined by the timpani and bongo drums, they seemed to keep toppling over on the many soloists, who could be heard only in bursts, like voices shouting into the wind. Among these all but submerged performers were Burt Collins, a pleasant, neo-bop trumpeter; Doug Mettome, a restless trumpeter who favors generous, legato swoops; Jimmy Cleveland, a masterly trombonist, who ripped off phenomenally rapid, burr-like strings of notes; and Gene Quill, an alto saxophonist, who shrilly emulated all the worst tonal aspects of Charlie Parker's style.

Although the Silver Quintet—Art Farmer, trumpet; Hank Mobley, tenor saxophone; Teddy Kotick, bass; Louis Hayes, drums; and the leader, piano—played with considerable heat, in the manner of many small modern-jazz groups, it sounded, in contrast to Richards' aggregation, somewhat like the Camp Fire Girls in song. Of its four extended compositions—all of them by Silver—perhaps the most striking was a rollicking blues, "Señor Blues," played in six-eight time, in which Silver, a dissonant and engagingly earthy pianist, and Farmer, a forceful, highly lyrical performer, produced an eloquence that seemed—partly, at least—the result of their restricting themselves to blessed everyday volume.

May 18

PASTORAL

JIMMY GIUFFRE, the gifted clarinettist, arranger, and composer, has made a new recording, "The Jimmy Giuffre 3" (Atlantic), that is a delightful jelling of many of his recent bold experiments with jazz rhythms and jazz themes. Although revolutionary, these experiments have had far less than an electric effect on modern jazz. For Giuffre's dulcet style of playing and the subtle, leafy structure of his writing have a deceptively timid, almost insulated quality, which is often ignored or shrugged off by the exponents of the beefier jazz experimentalism of such men as Charlie Mingus and Teo Macero. Giuffre's work is also elusive because of a characteristic he shares with an increasing number of his colleagues: he comes in two different parts—the highly inventive arranger-composer, and the accomplished instrumentalist. (Although he also plays the tenor and baritone saxophones, he has been concentrating in the past couple of years on a unique clarinet style. It is notable for its delicate vibrato, its simple legato phrasing, and the exclusive use of the lower and middle registers of the instrument, all of which produce a limpid, mahogany-colored sound.) This duality is, in some respects, even more marked in Giuffre than it is in other musicians; his instrumental style frequently seems a direct organic outgrowth of his compositions, and vice versa.

Giuffre, who is thirty-six years old and holds a degree in music, was one of the founders of the now declining West Coast school of modern jazz, a suave splinter movement that got started five years ago around Los Angeles and San Francisco. It produced, in the main, a glazed, dainty small-band jazz, which nevertheless brought to the fore excellent musicians like Giuffre, Shorty Rogers, Gerry Mulligan, and Shelly Manne. The movement developed, in addition to a rather sleek compositional approach—smooth unison ensembles, hushed dynamics, and sliding rhythm—an instrumental style very close to that of the cool school. At first, Giuffre's work seems the epitome of the West Coast method. Yet his playing has an urgent, if constantly veiled, lyric quality that suggests, rather than the bland variations of Shorty Rogers, the liquid but muscular work of such men as Jimmy Noone, Irving Fazola, and Pee Wee Russell. His arranging and composing have been equally independent of the West Coast school. In, for example, "Tangents in Jazz: The Jimmy Giuffre Four" (Capitol), a remarkable recording produced two years ago, Giuffre—in company with Jack Sheldon, trumpet; Ralph Peña, bass; and Artie Anton, drums—dropped the customary steady sounded beat completely and employed the rhythm instruments as semi-melodic, almost harmonic devices that both underscore and liberate the melody instruments. As Giuffre says in his notes for this record:

> I've come to feel increasingly inhibited and frustrated by the insistent pounding of the rhythm section. With it, it's impossible for the listener or the soloist to hear the horn's true sound . . . or fully concentrate on the solo line. . . . The essence of jazz is in the phrasing and notes, and these needn't change when the beat is silent. Since the beat is implicit, this music retains traditional feeling; not having it explicit allows freer thinking.

The over-all effect is that of loping freedom; the horns seem to coast effortlessly in and out of both the written and improvised passages, which are frequently broken by rests that are filled by the bass and drums with contrasting or imitative figures. (Giuffre often breaks up the standard thirty-two-bar chorus this way, and sometimes he abandons it for his own forms, of whatever length.) Although the implied beat occasionally seems—like a poised billy—more compelling than the steady thump of a bass drum, these rhythmic dalliances create a magic, free-ballooning setting for a second but equally important quality: the injection into much of the music of an elusive pastoral dimension. Two of the tunes, "The Leprechaun" and "Chirpin' Time," which are blues and folk in origin, have, because of Giuffre's clarinet and Sheldon's soft trumpet, a kind of evening, piper-in-the-meadow quality, a bucolic element that disappeared almost entirely from jazz in the twenties.

All this is buoyantly and intricately present in "The Jimmy Giuffre 3." Giuffre is accompanied by Jim Hall, guitar, and again by Ralph Peña. There are nine selections, seven of them by Giuffre. These are, nearly without exception, either unadorned blues or derived from blues. They are effectively broadened by the addition, here and there, of folk song and spiritual elements that appear both in the arranged passages, notably in "That's the Way It Is," and in the ad-lib playing, notably in "The Crawdad Suite," a tune in which Hall lets loose clusters of ringing chords that could easily have come from the late Leadbelly. "The Crawdad Suite" is a seven-minute composition built around two themes—an ingratiating blues and a haunting minor figure. The blues is played in a slow, steady rhythm, while the minor theme—which is stated sotto voce from time to time by the various players, as in a series of asides —has no rhythm at all. Both the blues and the minor theme are improvised upon (about half of the entire recording is written, though), and they are connected by short, lyrical passages, usually played by the guitar, that allow the two to follow one another like perfectly logical extensions. "The Train and the River" is a little descriptive piece, a refreshing idea that—except for rarities like Ellington's "Harlem Air-Shaft" and Meade Lux Lewis' "Honky Tonk Train Blues"—has largely been ignored in jazz. Giuffre embellishes the lively melody successively on the clarinet and two saxophones, while Peña and Hall work out train-like rhythms, which add to Giuffre's suggestion, on his tenor saxophone, of the melancholy wail of the steam whistle. Although there are, of course, never more than three instruments at work simultaneously, Giuffre manages—through the deft use of such devices as the constant varying of instrumental combinations (clarinet with bass, baritone saxophone with guitar, and so on), a fragile, intense counterpoint, and the occasional insertion of bits of fugue—to develop a multiplicity of sounds that would do credit to a ten-piece group. The playing is faultless. Hall is a young, no-nonsense guitarist who has much of the spare deliberation of Charlie Christian, and Peña is a forceful, big-toned performer. Giuffre matches their combined strengths with gentlemanly ease.

May 25

HOT

Roy Eldridge, a fiery and indefatigable trumpeter, makes it plain in a new recording, "Swing Goes Dixie" (American Recording Society), that he has lost none of the crackling excitement that has distinguished his work for the past twenty years. Few jazz trumpeters—even the young Louis Armstrong—have achieved Eldridge's pure, graceful hotness. Yet he is often academically dismissed as being merely the connecting link between Armstrong, who unwittingly formed the style of almost every trumpeter (Eldridge included) of the twenties and thirties, and Dizzy Gillespie, who, in turn, influenced (after a brief period as an admirer of Eldridge) almost every trumpeter of the forties and fifties. Eldridge is, however, far more than a transitional agent, for he is a highly original musician whose dignity and intense inventiveness are, at times, peerless. His style is wild and dancing and nervous, he seems to bite at, instead of merely blow, his notes, which rise in sudden, breathtaking swoops to the upper registers of his instrument or plummet to the low registers, where he often achieves a bleary, guttural sound. Eldridge also possesses a gift that is rare among jazz musicians; at his best—his unruly imagination now and then outruns his sizable technique—his solos are marvels of spontaneous construction, which march with a steady, unbreakable logic from oblique, studied beginnings to soaring, hats-off climaxes.

When this happens, one gets the impression that Eldridge has exhausted for all time the melodic potential of the material at hand.

The congenial group he works with on this recording includes Benny Morton, trombone; Eddie Barefield, clarinet; Dick Wellstood, piano; Walter Page, bass; and Jo Jones, drums. The title of the album is misleading, for, rather than being Dixieland—a clanging, head-on, small-band jazz played in the late twenties and the early thirties —this is an informal, unclassifiable type of jazz that was audible before and during the Second World War at occasional recording dates and at legendary after-hours jam sessions. There are eight selections, all of them Dixieland tunes. Eldridge is most eloquent in "Tin Roof Blues" and "Jada," in which he solos with a majesty that one expects not in jazz but in opera. Morton, Barefield, and Page, who are of Eldridge's generation and style, are competent, and so is Wellstood, but Jones is superb, for he performs with a stomping exhilaration he has never before revealed on records. His work behind Eldridge's first solo chorus in "Royal Garden Blues" is a classic bit of rocketing jazz drumming.

Jimmy Rushing, the suave, blimp-sized blues shouter, has always sounded as if he were wearing spats and morning coat and had just had a good laugh. His supple, rich voice and his elegant, almost Harvard accent have the curious effect of making the typical roughhouse blues lyric seem like a song by Noel Coward. In his most recent recording, "The Jazz Odyssey of James Rushing Esq." (Columbia), he is accompanied, with varying effectiveness, by four groups, all headed by Buck Clayton, a trumpeter who worked with Rushing for many years in the Count Basie band. The personnel also includes Vic Dickenson and Dickie Wells, trombones; Buddy Tate, tenor saxophone; Hank Jones, piano; and, again, Jo Jones. Four of the twelve numbers, among them "Rosetta" and the infectious " 'Tain't Nobody's Biz-ness if I Do," are blues, and it is on these that Rushing, who pauses frequently for wonderful solos by Clayton, Tate, and Dickenson, is in his gracious, and occasionally mournful, prime. There is also a rare and ingratiating piece of authentic Americana, "Tricks Ain't Walkin' No More," in which Rushing, accompanying himself on the piano, delivers a mischievous monologue on the waywardness of urban low life. The album cover, done in tempera by Thomas Allen, showing Rushing, in a red shirt, black suit, and battered panama, hustling off to New York, is perfect.

The baritone saxophone is an obtuse instrument. But both Harry Carney, who has been the foundation of the Ellington band since the Coolidge administration, and Gerry Mulligan have mastered its thick, lumpish sonorities, and Serge Chaloff, a contemporary of Mulligan's, handles the instrument with an equal and almost alarming agility. He exudes an unashamedly broad lyricism, based on a rich tone and an astonishing vibrato that beats even the celebrated vibrations of Sidney Bechet, the New Orleans clarinettist and soprano saxophonist. A ceaselessly restless player, Chaloff darts from frank, bumptious bass notes to soft, breathy high ones that barely get out of the loudspeaker. "Blue Serge" (Capitol), a fresh, relaxed recording with an inspired accompaniment—Sonny Clark, piano; Leroy Vinnegar, bass; and Philly Joe Jones, drums—is, all in all, probably the most satisfying one Chaloff has done. Clark and Jones are particularly stimulating, and a refreshing structural device is used here and there in the four-bar breaks that adds a light, surprised air to the proceedings: each man, in his turn, plays *a cappella.* There are seven selections, ranging from a sprightly blues to "Thanks for the Memory," "Stairway to the Stars," and "I've Got the World on a String," all of which Chaloff converts into a series of fervent arabesques that would edify their composers.

June 1

AVAUNT

AFTER SIXTY-ODD YEARS, jazz has finally established a set of traditions firm and tweedy enough to bring about what is—with the possible exception of certain pioneering efforts by Duke Ellington and Lennie Tristano—its first avant-garde movement. One of the leaders of this revolution, which includes such men as Charlie Mingus, John Lewis, Gerry Mulligan, and Jimmy Giuffre, is Teddy Charles, a militant and talented twenty-nine-year-old arranger, composer, and vibraphonist, who has been chiefly responsible in the past couple of years for an illuminating series of experimental recordings and concerts that have dealt largely with the slippery problem of making jazz composition as interesting as jazz improvisation. Although most of the compositions Charles has played call for standard jazz instrumentation, they depend rather heavily on such classical devices as atonality, polytonality, and frameworks of varied length. These innovations sometimes have a fairly somber effect, for they tend to bury the customary emotional content of jazz beneath a variety of formidable intellectual superstructures. As a result, Charles' music often has a juiceless Mozartean air—cool, dry, and tense. This is the result, as well, of Charles' precise, metallic playing and the inevitable difficulty the musicians who work with him have in remaining relaxed when confronted by unwieldy materials. A few evenings ago, Charles took part in a concert in the Contemporary Jazz/Composers' Series, at the Carnegie Recital Hall, and it was, in comparison with earlier recitals he has been involved with, a surprisingly brittle affair, distinguished by its mechanical enthusiasm and by the curiously flat, arch manner of many of the compositions.

The musicians—Idrees Sulieman, trumpet; Teo Macero, alto and tenor saxophone; Mal Waldron or Hall Overton, piano; Bob Prince or Charles himself, vibraphone; Addison Farmer, bass; and Jerry Segal, drums—performed in varying combinations, and all but Farmer and Segal contributed one or two of the eleven new pieces heard, which included a couple by a non-performer, John Ross. They ran, on the average, ten minutes, and they seemed, with three notable exceptions, pretty much alike—as if, in fact, they were all part of one huge composition that had been arbitrarily cut into sections. The exceptions, however, were completely engrossing—a slow ballad by Ross, "Ted's Twist," which had an extremely long chorus and a stately, attractive melodic line; "Take Three Parts Jazz," an ambitious venture by Charles, with a complex structure full of abrupt shifts from idyllic passages to sharply rhythmic ones; and "Tension," by Waldron, which used explosive, contrasting introductory figures, played alternately by trumpet and drums, and a taut, compelling, contrapuntal ensemble, filled with effective dissonances. The other pieces ranged from "Threnody," by John Ross, a long, cramped piece, apparently played almost without improvisation and that balanced brief solo flights against discordant ensembles, to Macero's heated "Conference with D.B.," which ended with lacy, upper-register piano notes pitched against the tinkling of Egyptian finger cymbals.

Charles, who carried the weight of the solo work, performed with his usual taste and fleetness. Of the pianists, Waldron was the more striking. In contrast to Overton, whose playing was as thin as tissue paper, he kept running up big, dark chordal structures that, perhaps because of the generally oblique turn of the music, never seemed conclusive. Sulieman, a flaring, rapid-fire trumpeter, fluffed a good many notes, and Segal, though an invariably steady performer, managed to make his drums sound as resonant as a battery of hatboxes. Macero, an emotional musician who in his most red-faced moments emits a variety of gasps, bad notes, and screeches, played with gusto, which occasionally lent the proceedings a welcomely fractious atmosphere, as if something exciting were about to happen.

June 8

COLOSSUS

POSSIBLY THE MOST incisive and influential jazz instrumentalist since Charlie Parker is a twenty-seven-year-old tenor saxophonist named Sonny Rollins, whose bossy, demanding style has made him the unofficial leader of a new and burgeoning school of modern jazz known as hard bop. Most of the members of the movement, which includes Horace Silver, Sonny Stitt, and Art Blakey, came to the front during the height of bebop, and as a result they largely formed their styles on Parker, Dizzy Gillespie, Lester Young, and Bud Powell. At the same time, they absorbed much of the nervous hotness of this music, which—though often regarded as an unduly complex type of jazz, what with its extended melodic lines, broadened chord structures, and jerky, rhythmic base—in many ways was a direct return to the pushing, uncomplicated vigor of Louis Armstrong's Hot Five. Rollins, who continues to use standard bop frameworks and instrumentation, has, however, developed a solo style that makes bop sound as placid as Handel's "Water Music." At first, there is something almost repellent about his playing, for his bleak, ugly tone—reminiscent, at times, of the sad sounds wrestled by beginners out of the saxophone—is rarely qualified by the gracefulness of a vibrato or by the use of dynamics. He seems, in fact, to blat out his notes as if they were epithets, and his solos often resemble endless harangues. After a time, though, it becomes clear that most of this staccato braying is a camouflage for a tumultuous and brilliant musical imagination and a rhythmic sense that probably equals Parker's.

Rollins is in his fearful prime in a new recording, "Saxophone Colossus" (Prestige), with Tommy Flanagan, piano; Doug Watkins and Max Roach, drums. Of the five numbers on the record—three are by Rollins—the best are "Moritat," from *The Threepenny Opera,* which he turns into a surprising combination of the brusque and the tender, and Rollins' "Blue Seven," a long, medium-tempo blues that features, in addition to his brooding variations, a remarkable solo by Roach, in which he ticks off on every part of his equipment a compelling, metronomic series of beats, the difficult tempo notwithstanding. Flanagan is a delicate, pearly-sounding pianist and Watkins is a firm bassist. Both manage to be more than foils for Rollins' red-necked vigor.

Thelonious Monk, the extraordinary and iconoclastic pianist and composer, has made a recording, "Brilliant Corners: Thelonious Monk" (Riverside), that is as provocative as any he has produced in recent years. In three of the five numbers he is joined by Ernie Henry (alto saxophone), Rollins, Oscar Pettiford (bass), and Roach, and in one by Clark Terry, Rollins, Paul Chambers (bass), and Roach. The fifth, "I Surrender, Dear," is an unaccompanied piano solo. The rest of the tunes, in all of which Monk had a hand, are, like his earlier ones, queer, moody, humorous compositions (dissonant, bumping ensembles, a variety of subtle rhythms, and an over-all needling piquancy), and they have a tortuous, concentrated power that produces a curious effect: the soloists, no matter how vigorous, seem secondary to their materials. As a result, although Rollins plays with much of his customary vibrancy, there is a subdued air about his work that fortunately balances the frenetic saxophone of Henry who, at his calmest (in an ingratiating blues called "Ba-lue Bolivar Ba-lues-are"), plays in a wild, chanting fashion. Monk is superb in "I Surrender, Dear," in which, free of a rhythm section, he produces a straggling army of flatted chords and off-notes that continually poke at and prick the melody. Chambers and Pettiford are satisfactory, but Roach occasionally becomes so energetic behind the soloists that he appears to be uncontrollably soloing rather than providing sympathetic support.

There is something invulnerable about a large number of brass instruments. In a recent recording, "Trombone Scene" (Vik), no less than eight modern trombonists—Jimmy Cleveland, Urbie Green, Frank Rehak, Sonny Russo, Eddie Bert, Willie Dennis, Jimmy Knepper, and Tommy Mitchell, who are accompanied by Elliot Lawrence, piano; Burgher Jones, bass; and Sol Gubin, drums—sing and roar, in solo and ensemble, with admirable effect. Each of the trombonists but Mitchell solos in one or another of the ten selections, and they are all excellent; Cleveland and Urbie Green, who plays with a soft, earnest assurance, are in superior form. The arrangements (most of them by Lawrence, who also provides an infectiously rumbling accompaniment on the piano) display a casual charm that continually buoys up the soloists.

"Trumpets All Out" (Savoy) is a similar but not nearly so successful recording, in which five trumpeters—Art

Farmer, Emmet Berry, Charlie Shavers, Ernie Royal, and Harold Baker—and a rhythm section deliver a series of generally shining solos, despite the rather skinny, unimaginative settings provided by Ernie Wilkins, an arranger and composer. Baker, an almost neglected performer who, like the late Joe Smith, has a serene, cowlike tone, is the most rewarding soloist, particularly in a husky, poignant version of "All of Me." Farmer is almost as persuasive. Shavers, however, who often plays as if he were a highly vitamined Harry James, jars against the prevailing atmosphere of subtlety and sensitiveness.

The American Recording Society, a record club with uncompromising standards, has just released "Johnny Hodges and the Ellington All-Stars," a recording that features nine of the present members of the Ellington band (Hodges, Clark Terry, Ray Nance, trumpet and violin, Quentin Jackson, trombone, Jimmy Hamilton, clarinet, Harry Carney, Billy Strayhorn, Jimmy Woode, bass, and Sam Woodyard), playing a soothing mixture of tunes like "Take the 'A' Train," "Black and Tan Fantasy," and "Just Squeeze Me" in the exact fashion of the various small Ellington groups of fifteen or so years ago, and with just as much warmth, humor, and intelligence. This is a delightful recording.

June 15

DJINNI

When Art Tatum, the miraculous, almost totally blind pianist, died last fall, at the age of forty-six, he was widely considered the greatest of all jazz pianists. This universal regard, however, has been at least partly created by the ballooning powers of a legend that confused his massive technique with his somewhat average abilities as a jazz improviser, and that got its start when Tatum appeared in the early thirties as the first full-fledged virtuoso performer that jazz had produced. In any case, the astonishment at his style—smooth, whipping arpeggios that seemed to be blown up and down the keyboard; impossibly agile bass figures; and furious tempos played with perfect touch —was deep and apparently permanent. For the rest of his life, Tatum continued to receive more attention than the average jazz musician, perhaps because he worked largely as a bravura solo pianist, whose surging orchestral approach never fitted into the collaborative confines of a jazz band. When he played with other musicians, an embarrassing thing happened: no matter how resolute his cohorts, he inevitably overran them; even while supplying accompaniment, he never seemed able to keep himself from swelling up, like an enormous djinni, alongside the soloist. Thus, Tatum was practically forced to establish his own medium of expression. His technique, which may have been equal to that of any pianist who ever lived, was, of course, based in jazz, but it was so superior to the standard popular songs he invariably used—peculiarly, Tatum never wrote a single tune—that it often took on a palpable life of its own, in the manner of the flawless execution of, say, a Salvador Dali. A fantastic embellisher, Tatum used the melody at hand not as a basis for improvisation but as an outline, which he would clothe with unique rococo rhapsodies of runs, breaks, and chords that at times seemed—because of their essential similarity—as if they could be transplanted intact from number to number with identical results.

Some of Tatum's brilliant cavorting is evident in a new recording—"The Art Tatum Trio" (Verve), made not long before his death, with Red Callender, bass, and Jo Jones—which is, compared to some of his other late work, a fairly docile effort. (A few years ago, in a set of a dozen or so Clef records, called "The Genius of Art Tatum," the pianist, unaccompanied, set down his ruminations on more than a hundred standard selections, in which he developed, again and again, elaborate clouds of sound that departed completely from an explicit beat and lasted for minutes at a time.) Tatum's bustling attack can, however, be heard here in "Just One of Those Things" and "Trio Blues," the latter of which he converts into a sly, though always gracious, parody of the blues. While Callender plays with aplomb throughout (there are ten selections in all), Jones fearlessly provides—in addition to a couple of stunning solos with the wire brushes that override Tatum's creeping, vinelike background figures—an almost governing support, which suggests that if Tatum had played with more musicians of Jones' strength, he might in time have pocketed some of his insuperable fireworks and got down to business.

Another new recording, "The RCA Victor Jazz Workshop: George Russell and His Smalltet" (Victor), is one of the most articulate, well-scrubbed, and uncompromising offerings to date by a member of the steadily growing school of modern jazz composers. The record presents twelve of Russell's compositions. They are played faultlessly by Art Farmer; Hal McKusick, alto saxophone and flute; Bill Evans, piano; Barry Galbraith, guitar; Milt Hinton or Teddy Kotick, bass; and Joe Harris, Paul Motian, or Osie Johnson, drums. The result is a series of dry, tight, and intricate pieces—two of them appear to be completely written and the rest both written and improvised—that use unsparingly such devices as 6/4 rhythm, shifting tonal centers, dissonant counterpoint, and a soloist improvising in one key against a background written in another. Although there are a good many excellent solos squeezed in between the written passages—Evans, a young pianist who plays with uneven but exhilarating force, and Farmer are the most rewarding—the over-all effect is starchy and convoluted. Often enough the writing, with its abruptness and its crackling discords (in "Round Johnny Rondo" there are a couple of arranged sections in which the trumpet and alto saxophone engage in a jarring and disconcerting counterpoint that resembles a badly out-of-focus photograph), doesn't seem to have much relation to the improvisation, and at times it even comes dangerously close to a highly skilled travesty of jazz that might have been cooked up, in anger and condescension, by someone who despised the music.

Even in the best of hands, the French horn is apt to emit a kind of strangled, mauve sound. An exception is the adroit work of a thirty-five-year-old musician named Julius Watkins, who appears in a recent recording, "Four French Horns Plus Rhythm" (Elektra), in company with three other French-horn players (David Amram, Fred Klein, and Tony Miranda), an accordionist (Mat Mathews), and a rhythm section (Joe Puma, guitar, Milt Hinton, and Osie Johnson). The record, which consists of three standard tunes and six original ones, is full of admirable things—a pinging Spanish guitar pitted against the four horns; muted ensemble choirs that produce far-off, bovine sounds; and the soaring solos of Watkins, who often darts restlessly and easily into the highest register of his instrument and plays at all times with a compelling and unfailing rhythmic sense. Fortunately, Mathews, a Dutch accordionist, avoids all the trembling, beery sounds usually associated with his instrument, and is, in fact, capable (in "Come Rain or Come Shine") of constructing solos that have both wit and considerable emotional weight.

The celebrated Dave Brubeck is a melodramatic pianist who sometimes tops even the magniloquence of Wagner. On a new and surprisingly restful recording, "Jazz Impressions of the U.S.A.: The Dave Brubeck Quartet" (Columbia)—made with Paul Desmond, alto saxophone, Norman Bates, bass, and Joe Morello, drums—he plays eight discreet and hummable compositions (one is an unaccompanied piano solo) that he wrote as evocations of various phases of a recent nationwide tour. In the notes on the record cover, Brubeck says of a tune called "History of a Boy Scout": "It is a mixture of humor and reverence that is so typical of the American G.I. It contains some of the skyrocket spirits of a Fourth of July parade, but there is an undercurrent of hallowed respect for the men of Valley Forge, Gettysburg, Ardennes, Wake, the Bulge, and Korea." As if that weren't enough, Morello, an exceptional young drummer who lately joined Brubeck, contributes masterly support, and, in "Sounds of the Loop," takes a four-minute solo that should not be missed.

July 13

MAMMOTH

THE MOST IMPRESSIVE thing about the four-day Newport Jazz Festival, which was held over the Fourth of July weekend in a lake-sized sports arena in Rhode Island, was its bulging, General Motors proportions. There were, in all, seven long concerts (four in the evening and three in the afternoon), at which no less than forty groups of performers—plus a couple of discussion groups—held forth before, altogether, between forty and fifty thousand people. Yet in all this vast and steamy musical circus, perhaps only a dozen musicians and singers performed with any real impetus and inspiration—a situation that quite possibly came about because most of the extraordinary number of musicians who appeared had to play at a dead run in order to avoid being trampled by the next group. The rest of the Festival was occupied by such things as a long and vapid performance by Louis Armstrong and his small band, which delivered, in a manner that was close to unintentional self-caricature, a program that has become as unalterable as the calendar; a series of interpretive jazz dances by Eartha Kitt and three members of the New York City Ballet, with accompaniment by Dizzy Gillespie's big band, that were, in addition to being disjointedly executed, without taste or point; and a confused and disrupted hour and a half by the Count Basie band, haphazardly augmented from time to time by such of its alumni and non-alumni as Jo Jones, Illinois Jacquet, Roy Eldridge, Sarah Vaughan, Lester Young, and Jimmy Rushing, the last of whom, nevertheless, kept ahead of his sloppy and blatant support.

The opening concert, on the evening of July 4th, purportedly a fifty-seventh-birthday celebration for Armstrong, was saved by the unassuming presence of George Lewis' band, an admirable seven-piece group that is one of the few genuine New Orleans-style bands still in existence. Although largely made up of near-octogenarians, it played with a sturdy and lively dignity that was most apparent in the long but continually absorbing ensemble passages and in the brief solos by Jack Willis, a trumpeter whose simple, classic playing had much of the neat lyricism of Tommy Ladnier. Jack Teagarden also propped the evening up by performing in several numbers with an uneven group led by Red Allen, which included Buster Bailey and J. C. Higginbotham, and in doing so proved that he has retained all his calm, lissome ways of singing and playing. Then Kid Ory, the great New Orleans trombonist, joined the group, and, though seventy now, puffed his way through "Muskrat Ramble" and "High Society" as if he were merely cooling his soup.

The other evenings were equally fitful. On Friday, Bobby Hackett conducted a six-piece organization that used, in varying combinations, such instruments as the alto horn, tuba, baritone saxophone, clarinet, and vibraphone, and that attempted, largely through rich, arranged ensemble passages, to chart an intrepid course between small-band swing and the early cool recordings by Miles Davis and Gerry Mulligan. Their playing was impeccable, but the result was damaged by the amplification system, which not only added an otherworldly humming sound to the instruments but tended to magnify their sound individually in the ensemble parts instead of reproducing it collectively. Erroll Garner, that indomitable pianist, gave a spirited, professional performance, with rhythm accompaniment, and a unit composed of, among others, Roy Eldridge, Coleman Hawkins, Jo Jones, and Pete Brown, an alto saxophonist, was notable for the ringing, declarative work of Hawkins. They were succeeded by Stan Kenton's newest big band, which brayed at the moon for at least an hour. On Saturday night, after a sparkling, if glancing, appearance by Teddy Wilson's trio, the Gerry Mulligan Quartet (his assistants were Bob Brookmeyer, Joe Benjamin, and Dave Bailey) put on a performance that, though excellent, was thin in comparison with the efforts of his recent and ingenious sextet. After its struggles with Miss Kitt and several inconclusive selections in which Mary Lou Williams, a masterly and semi-legendary pianist, was the soloist, Dizzy Gillespie's band roared raggedly on by itself and, at least in "School Days," sounded as if it really meant business. The final evening began—and to all intents and purposes ended—with the remarkable Jimmy Giuffre 3 (Giuffre, Jim Hall, Ralph Peña), which on top of absurdly having to provide quieting-down music for the late-arriving audience, was allowed approximately twenty minutes onstage.

Although the afternoon sessions were longer and even

more heavily populated by musicians, they were occasionally delightful. On Friday, Ruby Braff, the trumpeter, led an octet that included Pee Wee Russell, the trombonist Jimmy Welsh, and the pianist Nat Pierce through four pleasantly and simply arranged selections that offered exceptional solos by Braff and Russell; in "Nobody Else but You," Russell took a gentle, barely audible low-register solo that was the equal of any improvisation during the whole weekend. The following afternoon included short but characteristically impassioned performances by Eddie Costa, a young pianist who hammered out, with the help of a rhythm section, an exhilarating version of "Get Happy," and the Cecil Taylor Quartet (Taylor, Steve Lacy, Buell Neidlinger, and Dennis Charles), an atonal group whose complex and thoughtful dissonances seemed less cloistered and academic in the hot sun. The Farmingdale High School Dance Band, from Long Island, a fourteen-piece group whose average age was fourteen, ran through eight numbers that ranged from Basie's "Taps Miller" to an intricate modern piece, and did them all with an ardor, precision, and barefoot bounce that were irresistible. The principal soloist, an alto saxophonist named Andy Marsala, who is not related to the Marsala brothers, played—with a stone face—exactly as if he were Charlie Parker.

Sunday afternoon was given over to gospel singing. The first half of the concert involved the Clara Ward Singers, a lively but somewhat affected group; the Back Home Choir, a fifty-voice group that performed with volume and conviction; and the Drinkards, most of whose numbers were built around the swooping, shouting—and fascinating bodily contortions—of Judy Guions, who sang with a fervor that was hair-raising. Then, Mahalia Jackson, the stately gospel singer, whose very presence on a stage is awesome, delivered well over a dozen selections, accompanied by piano and organ, with an eloquence that led a swaying, front-row spectator to moan repeatedly, "Say it, 'Halia! That's right, say it now!"

July 20

THE M.J.Q.

IN THE THREE YEARS since its formation, the Modern Jazz Quartet, which is made up of John Lewis, piano; Milt Jackson, vibraphone; Percy Heath, bass; and Connie Kay, drums, has become, along with Gerry Mulligan's various groups and the Jimmy Giuffre 3, one of the most intelligent, stubborn, and cheering of all modern-jazz groups. Most contemporary small-band jazz depends on stiff, bony ensemble passages, which are used only as terminal points for long strings of solos. But the Modern Jazz Quartet, although it has occasionally frittered away a good deal of its subtle, intense inventions in a delicate tangle of structural devices like the fugue and the rondo, has rejuvenated, in a sometimes brilliant manner, two of the earliest and most basic ingredients in jazz—collective improvisation and the blues, which were prematurely swamped in the nineteen thirties by the stentorian arrival of the big jazz bands and great individualists, like Louis Armstrong and Coleman Hawkins. The quartet's soloists, who are most often Jackson and Lewis, usually perform—because of the sensitive, close-knit nature of the group—more as temporary offshoots from tight, central frameworks than as independent improvisers stepping baldly off into space. When Jackson, who gets a rich, forceful, quavering tone from his instrument, solos, Lewis works out a clear but discreet secondary melodic line behind him that is sometimes so provocative that it unintentionally upstages Jackson. (Lewis has the rare gift among jazz pianists of being able to act both as a sympathetic and agreeably distorted echo of the soloist he is supporting and as a convenient source of choice phrases that the soloist, if flagging, can lean on.) Thus the group is always in a state of ready and easy counterpoint, where, in the busiest passages, all the performers seem to jostle each other graciously, like the occupants of a crowded royal box.

Aside from the consistent excellence of its playing, much of the success of the group is due to its leader, Lewis, who is also an exceptional composer and arranger. Although his playing—simple, single-note melodic lines that have a shy, crystalline quality, an almost inaudible left hand, and a calm, doilylike approach—has a deceptive, amateur air, he is an uncanny performer, who often puts together, from combinations of nearly childish figures, solos that take on the ring of classic improvisations. In addition, Lewis, who is thirty-seven and holds a couple of degrees in music, has few equals in contemporary jazz as a melodic composer. His melodies, which are usually derived from the blues, have a graceful melancholy that sticks fast in the mind, much in the manner of such simpler pioneering jazz compositions as "Royal Garden Blues" and "That's a Plenty." Two of them—"Django," written as a requiem for the late French guitarist Django Reinhardt, and "Two Degrees East, Three Degrees West"—have already become indestructible jazz tunes.

The quartet's new recording, "The Modern Jazz Quartet" (Atlantic), is crisp and uncluttered. In addition to Lewis' "La Ronde," a two-minute piece that offers some solo wire-brush work by Kay, and "Baden-Baden," a fast blues by Jackson and bassist Ray Brown, it consists of nine standard tunes, five of which form a ballad medley played as a single unit. "Bags' Groove" and "Baden-Baden" are perhaps the most forthright recordings the group has yet made. Both have simple structures and straightforward solos, while Kay, a superior drummer who generally uses the wire brushes, shifts forcibly to sticks. The quartet's collective approach is particularly apparent in "Between the Devil and the Deep Blue Sea." During Jackson's second solo, Lewis drifts in behind him with a series of queer, limping tremolo phrases that seem to nudge Jackson quietly and firmly along, as if otherwise he might falter and, in doing so, take the whole group down with him.

Modern jazz drumming appears to have become permanently set in the narrow, florid, and often insensitive patterns of Max Roach, who, in the past seven or eight years, has had as much influence on his instrument as Charlie Parker on his. A new recording, "Orgy in Rhythm: Art Blakey" (Blue Note), though a sometimes unruly, tobogganing affair, is a stirring exception to the staccato, typewriter insistence of the Roach school. Blakey, whose style is full of mushrooming cymbal sounds and tidal snare-drum rolls, is joined on the trap drums by Arthur Taylor, Specs Wright, and Jo Jones, the last two of whom occasionally take turns on the timpani. Also present are Ray Bryant, piano; Herbie Mann, flute; Wendell Marshall, bass; and a steaming Afro-Cuban rhythm section, made up of Sabu on the bongos and timbales, and four others, who rattle away on conga drums, timbales, maracas, the cencerro, and the tree log. Of the four numbers on the record, three are largely Afro-Cuban, and have opening and closing sections, which are chanted by Sabu and Blakey. In between are such things as Jones racketing along against a conga-drum background; sharp, rifle-like bongo drums pitted against the subterranean rumbling of the timpani; and, in a couple of places, three trap drummers playing vigorous unison figures with all the authority and noise of the millennium. Blakey takes a stunning solo in a number called "Toffi," and in "Split Skins" the Afro-Cuban drummers rest while Blakey, Taylor, and Jones work out intricate supporting and solo figures, not to mention a solo that is probably the best one Jones has recorded. Although the notes on the record help designate which soloist is which, it might be of some additional use to know that, in all the din, both Taylor and Wright produce identical heavy, clipped, rather wooden sounds, Jones a lighter, crisper, almost startled sound, and Blakey a muzzy, booming sound.

Prestige has reissued on one side of a twelve-inch long-playing record called "Walkin': Miles Davis All Stars," a recording made about three years ago, with Davis, trumpet; Jay Jay Johnson, trombone; Lucky Thompson, tenor saxophone; Horace Silver; Percy Heath; and Kenny Clarke, drums, all of whom play, in two extended blues—"Walkin'" and "Blue 'N Boogie"—some of the best jazz improvisation set down in the past decade. On the second side, Davey Schildkraut, alto saxophone, replaces Johnson and Thompson, and the results (there are three standard tunes), though far more dulcet, are only slightly inferior.

July 27

THE OLDEN DAYS

THE FIRST Great South Bay Jazz Festival, which was held a week or so ago in a spacious, open-sided tent in Great River, Long Island, was, almost without exception, a miraculously sustained event that produced, in the course of three evening and two afternoon concerts, some of the most eloquent and heartening jazz played since the days, a decade ago, when jazz was still offered as a joyous music. Many of the dozen groups appeared at least twice, and, after a time, the music took on a kind of unity that allowed Coleman Hawkins, for one, to be heard every day in every conceivable sort of tune and mood, ranging from an impassioned "Body and Soul" to a loose, stampeding, up-tempo "Rosetta." Moreover, the tent helped establish an often exhilarating bond between performers and audience; Sunday night, Charlie Mingus, the bassist, suddenly burst into a breathtaking, half-shouted, half-sung accompaniment to his solo on "Woody'n' You," and in answer to an exclamation from the audience, the venerable, bespectacled clarinettist Garvin Bushell broke off in the middle of one of his solos, bellowed "Yes!," and resumed playing with even greater fervor.

The Festival was opened on Friday night by a seven-piece group led by cornetist Rex Stewart and including such men as Bushell, Hawkins, Benny Morton, and Bill Pemberton, bass. Although its ensembles tended to be patchy and one-legged, the soloists displayed an invention that reached notable proportions in a gentle, almost carved passage by Stewart in "Lazy River," in a long, slow "Tin Roof Blues" with a muted, from-afar solo by Stewart that seemed to be seized and shaken to pieces by an angry, rolling counter-statement by Hawkins, and in the closing ensemble of "Basin Street," when Hawkins came up with a couple of abrupt, yearning figures that had the effect of a gospel shouter letting loose. Although the Horace Silver Quintet (Art Farmer, Cliff Jordan, tenor saxophone, Silver, Teddy Kotick, and Louis Hayes), played with its usual decisiveness, its members—except for Silver and Hayes—assumed such forlorn and empty-faced postures that they looked as if they might simply blow away. A half-dozen extended numbers by the Jimmy Giuffre 3 were capped by "The Train and the River," which was brought to a climax when Giuffre, playing the tenor saxophone, somehow produced—even more effectively than in his recent recording of the number—a poignant celebration of all the emotions ever evoked by steam-engine whistles.

Saturday afternoon, a downy performance by the Billy Taylor Trio, which included Earl May, bass, and Ed Thigpen, drums, was saved by the taut, expert work of Thigpen. The Lawson-Haggart Dixieland Band (Yank Lawson, trumpet; Cutty Cutshall, trombone; Peanuts Hucko, clarinet; Bob Haggart, bass; George Barnes, guitar; Cliff Leeman, drums) pumped through six numbers, including a loping, twelve-minute "Jeepers Creepers" that was enhanced by the unscheduled appearance of Gerry Mulligan, who came onstage like a kindly, supercharged Uriah Heep and played with a gusto not always apparent with his own groups. In between, there was an absorbing hour by the Charlie Mingus Jazz Workshop, in which such musicians as Bill Triglia (piano), Curtis Porter (alto and tenor saxophones), and Jimmy Knepper worked their way through three labyrinthine selections that included a blues played simultaneously in two keys; "Tia Juana Table Dancer," which rose, in its ensemble sections, to a dissonant, volcanic din that resembled some of the symphonic works written in Russia in the thirties in praise of such things as power plants; and "Dizzy's Mood," with a tricky passage during which the rhythm section slid into a kind of double-time waltz tempo.

Saturday evening was memorable. Aside from two satisfying appearances by a sextet that included Buck Clayton, Vic Dickenson, Hank Jones, and the indomitable and gracious Jimmy Rushing, it was devoted to a reunion of the Fletcher Henderson band, pieced out (where necessary) with a few ringers. Seventeen strong, the band—which was under the direction of Stewart, and offered, among others, J. C. Higginbotham and Benny Morton, trombones; Joe Thomas, Emmett Berry, and Paul Webster, trumpets; Bushell, Edgar Sampson, and Hilton Jefferson, saxophones; Bernard Addison, guitar; and Jimmy Crawford (an alumnus of the Lunceford band), drums—surged through more than a dozen numbers that suggested that the group had been dissolved only the week before. In addition to superior solos by Stewart, Hawkins, and Berry, the drumming of Crawford, and the nostalgic pleasure of hearing, straight from the horse's mouth, Henderson arrangements of "Down South Camp Meeting," "King Porter Stomp," and "Wrappin' It Up," there was the pleasure of listening to the singing way the band attacked its material, and this provided a remarkable contrast to many of today's big jazz bands, which suddenly seemed overboiled, cumbersome, and unimaginative.

Sunday afternoon was run through meditatively by the Marian McPartland Trio, augmented by Bud Freeman, Vic Dickenson, and Jimmy McPartland, and the Miles Davis Quintet, which included Sonny Rollins and Paul Chambers, and which was notable for a languishing rendition by Davis, playing a tightly muted trumpet, of "It Never Entered My Mind." But that night, all the energies that had been present during the weekend exploded. The Lawson-Haggart band and Rex Stewart's septet, joined at times by Roy Eldridge, Jimmy Rushing, and Sammy Price (piano), reappeared, and so did Mingus, now as a soloist accompanied by rhythm. Much of the evening was given over to the blues. Two priceless things occurred: Mingus put so much emotion into a blues called "The Haitian Fight Song" that, peculiarly, his instrument became a totally inadequate medium for all it was forced to do; immediately after Rushing's first choruses of "Good Morning, Blues," Eldridge, who had been playing unevenly until then, slipped without warning into a triple-time tempo and, sotto voce, in the highest register of his instruments, delivered a solo chorus quite possibly as brilliant as any ever played.

August 3

COOTIE

UNHAPPILY, most admirers of jazz still appear to be governed either by a short-winded faddism that selects its youthful heroes on a kind of musician-of-the-month basis or by an academic approach that sets up in bronze and stone musicians who haven't played a fresh, honest note in fifteen years. As a result, a steadily diminishing number of middle-aged men, such as Ben Webster, Jimmy Rushing, Coleman Hawkins, Ike Quebec, and Jimmy Crawford, have, caught in the vacuum between these two groups, gone largely unnoticed since the mid-forties, although their faculties and inspiration remain demonstrably unimpaired. (Crawford, one of the ablest of all big-jazz-band drummers, has been pumping away in Broadway pit bands for years.) These melancholy thoughts have been touched off by a valuable new release, "Cootie & Rex in the Big Challenge" (Jazztone), which features Cootie Williams, the masterly, forty-nine-year-old trumpeter, in the first jazz recordings he has made in nearly a decade. Williams, of course, was one of the principal reasons for the success, in the thirties, of Duke Ellington and, in the early forties, of Benny Goodman. He perfected, under the influence of Bubber Miley, a trumpeter whom he replaced in Ellington's band, a still unsurpassed handling of the plunger mute (the plain old plumbing utensil, minus its handle) that results in some of the unique sounds in music.

Williams generally plays in the middle registers and uses simple phrases, but when he applies the plunger, he produces an inexhaustible variety of sounds that include aching growls, yearning, ghostly wahoos, and tight, intimate effects that suggest a wordless language of sharp consonants and drawn-out vowels. By comparison, hearing his open-horn style is like emerging from a dense wood into a bright meadow, for with it he gets a pushing, majestic tone that has the resonance of at least two trumpets and that moves with ease from a gentle urgency to savage, shouting statements that could propel an army.

In addition to Rex Stewart, who employs a delightful, slightly diminished version of Williams' style—a thinner tone, a less certain technique, and a tendency to rely on a stock of cute phrases—the ensemble includes Bud Freeman, Coleman Hawkins, Lawrence Brown, J. C. Higginbotham, and a rhythm section made up of Hank Jones, Billy Bauer on guitar, Milt Hinton, and Gus Johnson on drums. They play five standard tunes, a composition by Stewart, and a blues. There is a good deal of unevenness in the record—the choice of tempos occasionally seems inept and both Higginbotham and Freeman are somewhat uncertain—but there are memorable things, too. One is "Alphonse and Gaston," in which Williams, in alternating choruses with Stewart, plays a muted chorus, a growl chorus, a delirious chorus with the trumpet valves half closed, and a plunging open-horn chorus. Another is the two eloquent duets between Hawkins and Williams—in the opening and closing sections of "Do Nothing Till You Hear from Me," and in the first chorus of "I Got a Right to Sing the Blues"—in which Hawkins noodles ferociously in the background while Williams, muted, plays the melody as if he were serving tea. Another is a sheet-tearing growl chorus by Williams in "I'm Beginning to See the Light," which makes his long absence from records seem unpardonable.

"Back Country Suite" (Prestige) is a graceful and original first recording by Mose Allison, a pianist and composer who is just twenty-nine. It includes, in addition to five unrelated selections, a long suite that celebrates the innumerable moods of the blues. Allison, who is competently accompanied by Taylor La Fargue on bass and Frank Isola on drums, has a direct, clean manner of playing that reminds one of Nat Cole. The suite is ten brief descriptive sketches ("Train," "Warm Night," "Saturday," and so forth), all of them straight blues or derived from blues and all of them apparently almost completely arranged rather than improvised. In the course of the work, Allison moves from the sort of deep-dish blues piano usually associated with Jimmy Yancey to several light, jigging uptempo dances. He even sings once, in a piping, skinny fashion. The composition is, however, more successful as a whole than in its parts; some of the pieces ("Spring Song" and "Highway 49") seem unfinished, and others ("Blues" and "January") might, if enlarged, allow Allison some needed elbowroom for improvisation. Nonetheless, this is an honest distillation of an ageless jazz form.

A fascinating new tour de force from the Coast, "Sonny Rollins Way Out West" (Contemporary), involves Rollins, the bass of Ray Brown, and the drums of Shelly Manne. Although all six numbers run five minutes or more (one runs over ten), Rollins performs with a consistent resourcefulness and vigor that would leave most of his contemporaries (who, even though they keep on playing, generally run out of fuel after their first two solo choruses) wheezing for breath. On such numbers as "I'm an Old Cowhand" and "Wagon Wheels," Rollins fashions choruses that are—regardless of his persistently goatlike tone and his abrupt, cantankerous phrasing—a clear indication of a striving toward an improvisational approach that is revolutionary, for it is based on a remarkable use of polyrhythms and it wrestles continually with a new, elastic phrasing that completely reshapes the accepted measure-by-measure patterns of the thirty-two-bar chorus, which Charlie Parker and Lester Young were the first to break down. Rollins will, for example, concoct a simple six-note figure, repeat it insistently, like a broken record, then catch the listener up with a long moment of silence before sliding off into a soft, dizzying run that may be alarmingly capped by a raucous bass note. Manne and Brown more than fill the holes opened up by such instrumentation, and, in their brief solos, come close to equaling Rollins' inspiration and agility.

August 17

HOT NIGHT, LITTLE LIGHT

Norman Granz's current Jazz at the Philharmonic tour opened last Saturday night at Carnegie Hall, and, in view of earlier JATP appearances, the concert was a surprisingly tepid affair. It was of little help that midway in the evening the hall suddenly seemed to run out of air, leaving a hot, sticky vacuum, which was intensified by the melancholy lighting. For the most part, this was restricted to one large, soft spotlight, which focused on each of the soloists in turn and left the other musicians stumbling inkily around as best they could. The proceedings were begun by a highly uneven eight-piece group made up of four tenor saxophonists (Lester Young, Sonny Stitt, Illinois Jacquet, and Flip Phillips) and a rhythm section that included Oscar Peterson, Herb Ellis, guitar, Ray Brown, and Jo Jones. Stitt, a lean, tall man, who was the first, and is still the best, of Charlie Parker's countless followers, played with spirit and assurance, matched only by Lester Young's initial eight bars of "These Foolish Things Remind Me of You," in which he created a memorable set of coasting, oblique variations. Most of the group's final selection, an extremely fast version of "Indiana," was given over to a long drum solo by Jones, a hypnotically graceful performer, who used both sticks and bare hands. Toward the end of it, while hitting a pair of flanking tom-toms, he began crossing and recrossing his arms with such rapidity that the ensuing blur gave the startling impression that he was casually waving a large, transparent fan.

The gloom in the hall seemed to thicken during four numbers performed by the Modern Jazz Quartet—John Lewis, Milt Jackson, Percy Heath, and Connie Kay. It played with a delicate limpness, which was briefly relieved by a slow blues, "Now's the Time," with distinguished solos from Jackson and Lewis, and by a nimble tune of Lewis' called "The Golden Striker." The first half of the concert was brought to a close by a group consisting of the Modern Jazz Quartet minus Jackson but augmented by Roy Eldridge and Coleman Hawkins. Although Hawkins played with a stirring doggedness, his solos tended to come out in an unaccustomed series of lumpy, almost blatant phrases. Eldridge, who was equally ill at ease for the first few numbers, warmed up perceptibly, however, and during the group's last tune he was bowling irresistibly along, top down and throttle open. During all this, the rhythm section, falling into its customary subtle intricacies, sounded as if it were performing by itself in an adjacent room.

After the intermission, the Oscar Peterson Trio (Peterson, Ellis, and Brown) rumbled aggressively through four tunes, and, joined by Jo Jones, played on as a rhythm section for Stan Getz and J. J. Johnson with such ardor that the two horns, operating in a cool, studied manner that occasionally bordered on the glacé, nearly sank out of hearing. Eldridge and Hawkins swelled the group for one number, and balance was restored until Jones abruptly allowed the tempo to sag so much that it seemed the selection might end as a slow drag. Ella Fitzgerald, whose clear, scrubbed voice is sometimes so finished that it takes on a blank perfection, sang half a dozen pieces backed by the same rhythm section, and afterward was joined in a fast "Stompin' at the Savoy" by the entire cast, which riffed ponderously away behind her. The last of her accompanists to reach the stage was Stan Getz, who, just as he was emerging from the Stygian backstage area, executed a kind of quick, ghostly buck-and-wing before strolling demurely up to join his colleagues. It was the most spontaneous act of the night.

September 21

THE THREE LOUIS

DECCA HAS ISSUED a hefty album, "Satchmo: A Musical Autobiography of Louis Armstrong," done up like a box of Christmas chocolates, that includes—in addition to some enormous photographs (Armstrong in his stocking feet, Armstrong fondling a cat), a plodding account of his career (Louis Untermeyer), and an oblique appreciation (Gilbert Millstein)—no fewer than forty-eight pieces of music. Forty-one were recorded within the past nine months, and the rest in the past decade. All but two are replayings of numbers he first recorded between 1923 and 1934. Each one is introduced by Armstrong himself, who, reading from an implausible script, occasionally sounds as if he were intoning the Kellogg-Briand Pact. There are some mediocre pieces, but the album also contains some of his most durable work. It comes at a fortunate time. A truly celebrated figure, Armstrong has recently begun offering in his public appearances little more than a round of vaudeville antics—clowning, bad jokes—and a steadily narrowing repertory.

Armstrong comes in several parts—the trumpeter, the singer, and the showman. As a trumpeter, he is one of the few jazz musicians whose careers have had the length and variety to be divided into distinct periods. The first began in the early twenties and ended around 1930. Playing in small New Orleans-style ensembles, he had an uncluttered, deceptively matter-of-fact manner that was marked by a brassy tone and a tendency to fluff one out of every five notes. But his basic style—a lyrical hugging of the melody and a rich, fervent texture—was already unmistakable. In the late twenties, he became the first of the great primitive jazz soloists. He abandoned the New Orleans style (Armstrong has never been a comfortable ensemble player, for he is apt, as if in a creative trance, to ignore what goes on around him), and for the next three or four years was a soloist in large, ragged, moaning groups. Despite the tea-dance backgrounds they generally gave him, he produced a series of solos, on such tunes as "Basin Street Blues," "That's My Home," and "I Gotta Right to Sing the Blues," in which, moving into the upper register, he perfected a soaring lyricism, full of swoops and falls, that still seems boundless. Since the mid-thirties, his style, hampered by an inevitable lessening of physical power, has become a mixture of his first two periods—short, simple, declamatory phrases placed end to end with uncertain, empurpling sorties into the high register.

Although Armstrong has for twenty-five years been regarded, because of his influence over his contemporaries, as a supernal figure, he has, at the same time, rarely seemed to extend himself beyond a straightforward use of his unique gifts. Never an energetic improviser, he has limited himself to direct, if sometimes unforgettable, embellishments. His technique is at best adequate. He has played a given solo nearly note for note year after year. And, most important, his emotional vigor has often peculiarly just missed getting through the broad assurance of his playing. For all that, he has invariably managed, as the purest of all jazz musicians, to be an infallible definition of just what jazz is.

Armstrong has always been a peerless jazz singer. His deep, dragging, first-sergeant baritone sounds as if it had been irreparably frayed from overuse, yet he handles a song with a sensitivity that converts it into a wholly new melody. (He has, however, never paid much attention to articulation or the sense of lyrics, which he generally reduces to an unintelligible rubble of long vowels and slurred consonants.) In fact, the agile, legato warmth of his voice has, in the long run, surpassed, in its imaginativeness and flexibility, the very trumpet playing he is principally revered for. It is quite possible, too, that Armstrong's stage presence—a heady and steadily revolving mixture of thousand-watt teeth, marbling eyes, rumbling asides, infectious laughter, and barreling gait—is as endearing a spectacle as we have had on the American stage.

Armstrong is accompanied for much of the first half of the album by his regular group (Edmond Hall, clarinet; Trummy Young, trombone; Billy Kyle, piano; Squire Gersh, bass; and Barrett Deems, drums), which plays a tenuous New Orleans style and is augmented here and there by George Barnes and Everett Barksdale, guitar, and Yank Lawson. It is spelled on several occasions by a couple of other groups, including such men as Jack Teagarden, Barney Bigard, Earl Hines, and Sidney Catlett. Among the tunes are many of the ones that Armstrong previously recorded with King Oliver's Creole Jazz Band and with his own Hot Five and Hot Seven. The present recordings—not counting an exceptional version of "King of the Zulus," a raucous "Snag It" (which he has never recorded before), and an intense "All the Wrongs You've Done to Me"—are inferior to the earlier ones. There are also, however, four blues, sung with earnest monotony by Velma Middleton, in which Armstrong acts as an accompanist, as he often did in the twenties for such singers as Ma Rainey and Bessie Smith. In two of them, "Reckless Blues" and "Court House Blues," he plays shaded, casual obbligatos—some so soft they can barely be heard—that are as effective as anything he has ever recorded.

The final half of the album concentrates on the years between 1929 and 1934, and, again, is mostly given over to Armstrong's present group, enlarged by a saxophone section. On tunes like "Lazy River," "Song of the Islands," "If I Could Be with You," and "I Surrender, Dear," Armstrong plays and sings with a lift and ease that at times remind one of his greatest period. Edmond Hall, who achieves a throaty, floating sound, is flawless throughout, and Young, an alumnus of the old Lunceford band, plays with more decorum and thought than he has shown recently. Both Kyle and Gersh are satisfactory, but Deems remains a soggy, punchy performer. He is, however, mercifully under-recorded.

September 28

STRESS AND STRAIN

One of the leaders of an increasingly fashionable school of modern jazz called—with equal opacity—"hard bop" or "funky" is Horace Silver, a thin, hard-working pianist, composer, and arranger of twenty-nine, who resembles an inverted, rapidly jiggling fishhook when he plays. In an ambitious new recording, "The Stylings of Silver" (Blue Note), Silver, in company with Art Farmer, Hank Mobley, Teddy Kotick, and Louis Hayes, demonstrates a good many of the rules and regulations of the movement. Its firmest is the homage the school gives the blues. Many of the compositions they play are straight blues or are based on the blues, and they usually sound as if they were attempting to resurrect the hot, grainy quality of old blues singers and pianists like Blind Lemon Jefferson and Jack Dupree. To this end, the hard boppers employ a heavy or sharply accented beat, a florid, staccato attack, and a hardness of timbre that is in direct contrast to the soft, inky sounds of the cool school. (Few of Silver's cohorts, though, have rejected one habit of the cool school —an affected boredom that is sometimes more noticeable than the music itself.) The instrumentation of the funky school is generally the one Silver employs, and its structure is time-honored—opening and closing ensembles, in which unison writing is often paramount, that form a container for the solos, which are occasionally of great length.

In fast tempos, these methods are apt to produce a metronomic feverishness that reminds one of the early Lunceford band. In slow tempos, curious things happen: the rhythm section, apparently unable to keep a relaxed beat, frequently slips into a disconcerting, ticlike double time behind the soloists, while the horns, seemingly incapable of developing the logical melodic flow of, say, Coleman Hawkins, tend to blurt and stagger. These peculiarities, combined with a sameness of dynamics and voicings, can result in a queer contradiction—the anxiety and energy the musicians devote to their work flattens out the very bearishness they seek into a rigid monotony.

One of the six selections on the record is a standard tune. The others, by Silver, are the most arresting pieces, melodically and structurally, that he has written. The complex and ingratiating melodic figure of "Soulville," a minor-key blues, is spun out over a chorus of three twelve-bar sections, which is broken by an eight-bar bridge. Another blues, "Metamorphosis," has an extremely long chorus (sixty-one bars) and a sixteen-bar bridge. Several of the tunes slip in and out of two-beat and beguine rhythms. Silver is a gifted pianist. His style, a first cousin to Thelonious Monk's, involves spare, reiterated, single-note right-hand figures that sometimes have the woodpecker tenacity of certain boogie-woogie patterns. They are offset by cautious little bumping figures in the left hand. All the musicians play with their customary zest, except perhaps Farmer, who sounds, in "No Smokin'," as if he were trying to ingest a vast number of peanut-butter sandwiches.

Farmer can be heard to far better advantage in the "Hal McKusick Quintet" (Coral), which contains the best work he has yet set down. In the past year, Farmer has become one of the few genuinely individual modern trumpeters. (Nine out of ten modern trumpeters are true copies of Dizzy Gillespie or Miles Davis.) His playing is an offshoot of the work of Davis as well as of that great Ellington alumnus Rex Stewart, and offers a round, chamois tone that stiffens only slightly in fast tempos, a highly selective variety of notes, each of them given equal thought. Together with McKusick, an alto saxophonist and clarinettist who bears a refreshing resemblance to Benny Carter (nine out of ten modern alto saxophonists are true copies of Charlie Parker), he plays ten selections, four of them new tunes and the rest standards. In most of them, Farmer and McKusick, accompanied by an excellent rhythm section (Eddie Costa, Milt Hinton, and Gus Johnson), move easily through partly contrapuntal ensembles that are most effective in "For Art's Sake," in which Farmer uses a mute and McKusick the bass clarinet, a deep, soothing instrument that has an irresistible lowing quality. All the solos are creditable, but Farmer takes an unforgettably poignant break at the start of his solo in "Gone with the Wind," first pausing for a couple of beats and then launching into a gentle, seven-note figure that has the motion of a slow, graceful dance.

Capitol has released "Gotham Jazz Scene: Bobby Hackett and His Jazz Band," by a group that offers the unusual instrumentation of cornet (Hackett), E-flat horn (Dick Cary), clarinet and baritone saxophone (Ernie Caceres), vibraphone and clarinet (Tom Gwaltney), and a rhythm section of piano, bass, tuba, and drums. The group handles Cary's ingenious arrangements with unflagging wit and vigor. Half of the eleven tunes are Dixieland numbers whose partly arranged ensembles give them a taut and tidy air. Two numbers—slow, richly textured pieces, full of dark voicings—are similar to some of the work done eight or ten years ago by the Miles Davis-Gerry Mulligan group. "In a Little Spanish Town" is a cheerful, stomping spoof, in which the principal ensemble figure, a souped-up version of the original, is delivered jointly by the tuba and a clarinet. It is punctuated several times by a wild bebop figure—from a tune called "Salt Peanuts"—played by the rest of the band. All the numbers are demonstrations of the way inspired ensemble passages, no matter how tightly structured, can send a soloist flying exuberantly into space. Hackett, who is often a blurred version of Bix Beiderbecke, has never before displayed such fire and bounce on records, and Cary, who has become a first-rate practitioner on his horn—a muffled cross between a French horn and a trombone—does a solo in a long and rambling rendition of "Tin Roof Blues" that is a model combination of lazy, soaring figures and nimble runs. Everyone else follows close behind.

October 26

MINGUS BREAKS THROUGH

"THE CLOWN" (Atlantic), a recent recording by Charlie Mingus, the redoubtable bassist and composer, is, despite its occasional freakishness, an even more exhilarating effort than "Pithecanthropus Erectus," made a year ago for the same label. It is one of the few recordings in which a modern jazz composer has successfully produced, through the blending of complex compositional devices with improvisation, that indispensable and ingenuous lyricism that survived in first-rate jazz until a decade ago. Most experimental jazz has been governed by a queer dilettantism of newness for newness's sake, and much of it has been little more than an agglomeration of classical technique pasted onto standard jazz contents. Mingus has allowed his forms to be primarily ordered by the highly original content of his music, and, unlike a lot of his contemporaries, who play as if at chess, he performs with an exuberant, sometimes unruly urgency that ignites both his compositions and the musicians who work with him.

Mingus, a large, shapeless man of thirty-five, belongs to no school of jazz. He has appeared with an extraordinary variety of musicians, including Kid Ory, Louis Armstrong, Duke Ellington, Red Norvo, and Charlie Parker. His playing has always reflected the easy lyricism of these men, and he is blessed with a superlative technique. He has an enormous tone, and a dexterity that enables him, for example, to repeatedly pluck one note so rapidly that it sounds like a sustained note, or to impart to a note the clarity and resonance of a drumbeat. In ensemble, he unreels unbroken countermelodic lines—most bassists simply supply the basic chords of the tune—while maintaining a thumping beat that leans slightly ahead of itself (like the drumming of Sidney Catlett), so that his cohorts are forcibly shunted along, both melodically and rhythmically. His solos are never displays of virtuosity. Occasionally, Mingus tends to belabor his instrument, as if it had attacked *him*, but at their best his solos contain a poignance that is unmistakable despite the essentially fuzzy, low-pitched properties of the pizzicato bass. Mingus' composing is equally strenuous. Often built around the particular talents of the musicians on hand—in the manner of Duke Ellington, whose methods appear in various shades throughout Mingus' work—it uses forms that grow directly out of his melodic ideas. In the notes for his new recording, Mingus says of the title piece, "The Clown": "I was playing a little tune on the piano that sounded happy. Then I hit a dissonance that sounded sad, and realized the song had to have two parts." Despite such haphazard and elementary beginnings, Mingus shapes his melodic inventions into an intricate harmonic system, which he describes in the notes to "Pithecanthropus Erectus":

> I "write" compositions—but only on mental scorepaper—then I lay out the composition part by part to the musicians. I play them the "framework" on piano so that they are all familiar with my interpretation and feeling and with the scale and chord progressions to be used.

Later, he says of a number called "Love Chant":

> This is an extended form version on a more or less standard set of chord changes. This form challenges the musician to create a line of long-held notes for the first chorus, to develop it on one or two chords (or rhythm patterns, scales, etc.) and then redevelop the line on the out chorus. This is done using only one or two chords per phrase so the lines must be developed for a much longer period of time than is usually taken before the chord change. . . . The whole success of extended form depends on the ability of the musicians to do this in soloing and also in playing counter or accompanying lines.

Thus Mingus, as a jazz composer, daringly asks of his musicians even more than the classical composer asks of his—that they carry both the letter and the spirit of the basic patterns of his composition over into their improvisations instead of conventionally using them as a trigger for their own ruminations. Still another characteristic of Mingus' writing is his peculiar preoccupation with program music. It is here that the experimentalist slides over into the showoff. In "A Foggy Day," which is in "Pithecanthropus Erectus," the Gershwin melody, though handled in a fairly straightforward manner, is delivered against a barrage of police whistles, simulated taxi horns, sirens, foghorns, and the sound of a docking ferry, done by Mingus on the bowed bass.

Mingus really lets go in his new record. There are four numbers, all by Mingus, who is joined by Curtis Porter, Jimmy Knepper, Wade Legge, piano, and Dannie Richmond, drums. Most of the tune called "The Clown," which lasts over twelve minutes, is an "improvised" narration, spoken with custardlike emphasis by Jean Shepherd, that deals with a symbolic clown who wants only "to make people laugh" but who gets the biggest laugh of his career when he is accidentally hit by a backdrop and killed. Fortunately, the narration is accompanied by and interspersed with some marvelous musical antics—comic trombone slurs, umpah rhythms, a waltz section, and a short, lovely melodic theme. The most striking number on the record, however, is a very long blues, "Haitian Fight Song." Though structurally demanding, it is one of the most unbridled blues ever recorded. Mingus introduces it on his bass with two clarion choruses that easily rival Louis Armstrong's opening of "West End Blues." He then shifts into a medium tempo and plays a brief, impelling rhythmic figure, which is gradually built upon by the rest of the musicians, who play with an increasing intensity and volume that reach a heads-off climax in a series of dissonant shrieks, an effect that is almost unendurably heightened by a weird whooping sound, like a wild, if muted, trumpet growl, presumably delivered, at the top of his lungs, by Mingus. The passage dissolves abruptly into the first solo, which, like many of the succeeding ones, is restlessly broken into four sections—medium tempo, double-time tempo, stop-time tempo, and again medium tempo. Many versions of the blues lope along like a determined walker, but Mingus' rhythmic and dynamic variations rub continually at the listener, as if they were arguments instead of music. "Blue Cee," another blues, revolves around an attractive melody and is capped by a weird ooh-wah figure, played partly in unison, partly in counterpoint, by the two horns. This starts off at a whisper, quickly reaches a howl, and then suddenly—when one is prepared for a demonic ending—subsides into a mournful lyric call.

Mingus' musicians are unruffled throughout. Porter is an adept, if somewhat conventional, student of Charlie Parker and Sonny Rollins. But Knepper, unlike most modern trombonists, who skate around on the glassy surface of J. J. Johnson's style, achieves here and there a rough, hustling quality that is reminiscent of the work, twenty years ago, of J. C. Higginbotham. Mingus is superb. His long solos in "Haitian Fight Song" and "Blue Cee" are—with their lightning combinations of fluttering, high notes, spacious intervals, and stentorian single notes broken by reverberative silences—great bass performances.

November 9

THE RESURGENCE OF RED ALLEN

IT HAS BEEN nearly thirty years since Red Allen, the tireless, sad-faced trumpeter, became one of the first practitioners of the instrument to move away from the blanketing influence of Louis Armstrong. Today, at the age of forty-nine, he is an unspoiled, non-repetitive musician who, astonishingly, is still widening his style. Allen left an identifiable mark on the early work of Roy Eldridge, who, in turn, influenced Dizzy Gillespie, the present champion of modern jazz trumpeters. Allen is erratic, restless, and highly lyrical. Sustained legato phrases that undulate like a calming sea are linked by jumpy connective passages —full of seven-league intervals and slightly flatted notes— that may or may not land on their feet. His thin, coppery tone occasionally softens, but more often it pierces straight to the bone. Once in a while, too, he ascends wildly into the upper register or relies on technical tricks, such as a rapid, birdlike tremolo, achieved by fluttering two valves up and down, that sound more difficult than they are. At his best, Allen is one of the most eloquent of jazz musicians. His melodic feeling is governed almost completely by the blues; he infuses just about every tune with broadly played blue notes. In the past few years, a remarkable thing has happened to Allen's playing. Unlike many of his contemporaries, who tend to ignore what has come after them, he appears to have been listening to modern jazz. The unsteady, staccato blare that has characterized his work now frequently gives way to a thoughtful, more generous tone and a myriad of soft glancing notes that resemble nothing so much as a nervous, vigorous Miles Davis.

Allen's rejuvenation is apparent in the recent "Ride, Red, Ride in Hi-Fi" (Victor), which contains nine numbers. Also on hand, among others, are Buster Bailey, J. C. Higginbotham, Coleman Hawkins, and Cozy Cole. The recording is exasperatingly uneven. The barely skeletal arrangements are climaxed a couple of times by meaningless grandstand codas, and a desperate, semi-burlesque number, "Ride, Red, Ride," is done at a flag-waving tempo full of boiling trumpet and a chorus of voices that chants the title. Both Bailey and Higginbotham are in uncertain form, and Cole, who usually combines a faultless technique with sensitive support, indulges in a door-slamming afterbeat that continually joggles the melodic flow. Nonetheless, in "Sweet Lorraine," "I've got the World on a String," and "I Cover the Waterfront," all taken at slow speeds, Allen produces long and memorable solos, in which he alternates judicious high notes with lush, booming, trombonelike phrases. He does not, however, top Hawkins, who has recently abandoned the cool, precise museum of tenor saxophonology that he had become ten years ago for a heated, angry style that suggests the work of a young, uninhibited imitator.

"Traditionalism Revisited" (World Pacific Records) is a relaxed recording in which Bob Brookmeyer, the youthful and adept nasal-toned valve trombonist who appears never to fluff a note, and Jimmy Giuffre, the mauve-sounding clarinettist, unpretentiously ease into their own idiom some of the numbers that Allen and Hawkins grew up with. (Their companions are Jim Hall, two alternating bassists, and a drummer.) There is, though, one pleasant bit of imitation; in the opening section of "Sweet Like This," Brookmeyer and Giuffre copy, almost note for note, two solos in the original King Oliver recording. Several of the tunes are associated with other musicians—"Louisiana" with Count Basie, "Some Sweet Day" with Louis Armstrong, "Truckin' " with Fats Waller—and are successful attempts to capture their melodic rather than their improvisatory possibilities. Thus, "Don't Be That Way" is turned into a slow, swaying number that contrasts sharply with the bristling foundry treatment usually accorded it by Benny Goodman's big band; "Sweet Like This," a plaintive blues, becomes a short, poetic idyll; "Ja-Da" is played in an oblique way, free of the stertorous bounce generally given it by Dixieland groups. In half of the eight tunes Brookmeyer switches to the piano, which he plays like a sleepy Thelonious Monk, while Giuffre shuttles back and forth between the clarinet and the tenor and baritone saxophones. The musicians' total immersion in their materials may be responsible for an accidental resurrection; during his solo in "Honeysuckle Rose," Hall slips in some chunky figures straight from the late Charlie Christian, and Brookmeyer immediately adds some rumbling, striding left-hand Basie figures. It is precisely the sort of collaboration Basie and Christian so often achieved on several of the old Goodman small-band records.

Victor has issued a puzzling record, "Dave Garroway: Some of My Favorites," on which Matt Dennis, a nightclub singer, walks through four undistinguished selections, surrounding four nearly perfect numbers by a Red Norvo group that includes (in addition to the celebrated vibraphonist) Ben Webster on tenor saxophone, Harry Edison on trumpet, Jimmy Rowles on piano, and bass and drums. All of their selections are slow, suave blues, one of them a first-rate re-creation of "Just a Mood," a languorous milestone first recorded in 1937 by Norvo, Harry James, Teddy Wilson, and bassist John Simmons.

Columbia has indulged in further confusion with the release, under a subsidiary label, of "Metronome All-Stars" (Harmony), which consists of nine of the historic All-Star recordings made between 1940 and 1950 by such men as Jack Teagarden, Dizzy Gillespie, Johnny Hodges, Count Basie, and Goodman. Comparison with the originals indicates that about half of the numbers are not the "takes" that were used for the original issues. Moreover, one number, "Dear Old Southland," has never been released before. Columbia has not bothered to supply any of this information.

November 30

HOT AND COLD

ALTHOUGH JAZZ has been more or less a fixture in concert halls for twenty years, it is commonly handled as if it were a run-down circus. The concerts almost always begin late, and, like any sideshow, are generally conducted by a master of ceremonies, who is often that pale descendant of the old circus barker, the disc jockey. Indeed, the music is usually buried in irrelevant words, both spoken and written. In addition to an m.c., there are frequently *two* printed programs, one free and one customarily a dollar, which are full of encomiums to performers who may or may not appear but rarely mention what is to be played—information that, like as not, doesn't come from the stage, either. The staging, at best, is informal: the lighting is apt to alternate between an overexposed blare and a mysterious twilight, and the microphones are often placed in such a way that if, say, a big band is performing, its soloists, for all that can be heard of them, appear to be engaging in pantomime. Many of these traditions were closely followed at a couple of concerts presented within the past ten days or so at Carnegie Hall. The most recent, titled "Thanksgiving Jazz," was held in marathon fashion last Friday evening—at eight-thirty and again at midnight. The early edition was opened half an hour late by Dizzy Gillespie's big band, which played eight numbers, including a fast, unidentified blues in which several unnamed soloists puffed, chests out, against the accompanying overmagnified explosions of the band, and lost; Gillespie's "Night in Tunisia," which had a long solo by Lee Morgan, a young trumpeter who showed more technique than imagination; and a howling up-tempo number, "The Champ," built around a drum solo, by Charlie Persip, that went on like the Great Plains. The band also dished up accompaniment for Ray Charles, a blues singer and pianist, who, apparently awed by his surroundings, at first offered a variety of timid and unoriginal piano solos on standard tunes, and then finally, as if in defiance, sang a raucous and moving version of "I Want a Little Girl," which startled the audience into its first big response of the evening.

Benefiting, perhaps, from a between-the-halves fight talk, things brightened considerably after the intermission. Thelonious Monk, who approaches a keyboard as if it had teeth and he were a dentist, appeared with a quartet (John Coltrane, tenor saxophone; Ahmed-Abdul Malik, bass; and Shadow Wilson, drums) and worked his way through five somewhat calculated numbers, which had such fearless titles as "Crepuscule with Nellie," "Nutty," and "Epistrophy." Coltrane, a hard-toned, uninhibited performer, took several solos, during most of which he relied on a series of complex dancing runs that seemed, nonetheless, more automatic than inspired. The program sagged momentarily during three arid numbers by a quintet led by Zoot Sims and Chet Baker, trumpet, who were accompanied by a rhythm section. They abruptly gave way to a stunning performance by Sonny Rollins, who was joined by bass and drums. Rollins is possibly the most courageous improviser since Charlie Parker, and in the course of three numbers—"Moritat," "I'll See You Again," and "Some Enchanted Evening"—filled the hall with a booming and far more lyrical tone than is his custom. His solos—in their combination of runs, weird, oblique statements of melody, and sly bits of wit—were masterpieces of their kind. Then Billie Holiday, who has lately shown signs of settling into an uncertain, stylized version of her former self, delivered seven songs with charm and assurance. There were, to be sure, times when her bent phrases and husky voice dissolved into flatness and sheer croak, but in most of her numbers she sang with lilt and lyrical invention. Some of this was due to her accompaniment, which, in addition to bass and drums, included Mal Waldron, who developed a steady flow of elastic countermelodies that seemed, at every turn, to sustain and point up Miss Holiday's voice. It was a memorable twenty minutes.

The earlier concert was also a double-decker, called "Jazz for Moderns," and its eight-thirty version turned out to be as moony and sluggish a demonstration of cool jazz as has ever been heard hereabouts. On hand were the Australian Jazz Quintet; Helen Merrill, a singer; the Miles Davis Quintet; the Gerry Mulligan Quartet; the Chico Hamilton Quintet; and a small, miscellaneous quintet led by the vibraphonist Lionel Hampton, a rather outlandish replacement for the scheduled George Shearing Sextet. The only indications that there was any life onstage occurred during Hampton's performance, and during two of the four numbers by Davis' group, which included Julian Adderley on alto saxophone, Tommy Flanagan, Paul Chambers, and Philly Joe Jones. In "Walkin'" and "Night in Tunisia," Davis, often a moody, hesitant performer, let loose a couple of belling solos that were spelled by some incisive drumming from Jones. In addition, one of Mulligan's numbers, "Storyville Story," became an aggressive blues in which the leader, who was accompanied by Lee Konitz, alto saxophone, and bass and drums, played the piano rather than his customary baritone saxophone. The rest of the evening, however, was taken up by a variety of sidling, tiptoeing sounds, made by such front-parlor instruments as the bassoon, the flute, the cello, and the vibraphone, as well as by Miss Merrill, who sang in a flat semi-whisper and handled her lyrics as if she were trying to invent a new language. The program was late in starting, and was conducted by a disc jockey named Symphony Sid, who spent a good deal of energy waggling the microphone around like a pilot's stick and plugging his new radio program, which apparently can be heard on both AM and FM.

December 7

PART THREE

1958

EPITAPH

THE FINAL COLLAPSE of the big-band era in the late forties left a permanent hole in jazz. The best of the big bands provided not only floating finishing schools for young musicians but the sort of roaring, imperious excitement that the small jazz group, for sheer want of volume, rarely matches. There were at least three distinct types of big band—the milky, unabashed dance band (Guy Lombardo, Charlie Spivak), the semi-jazz dance band (Tommy Dorsey, Artie Shaw), and the out-and-out jazz band (Duke Ellington, Fletcher Henderson). The demise of this small but lively industry was due largely to economics; it is also true that the big jazz band had just about run dry. It ended as it had begun—as a plump, highly regimented expansion of the traditional New Orleans instrumentation of cornet, clarinet, trombone, and rhythm section. There was not really much difference, for example, between the Goodman band of 1936 and the Woody Herman band of a decade later. Goodman had fourteen pieces and a mechanized, tank-like style, and Herman had four or five more sidemen and a loose, flag-waving approach, but both groups depended on the same basic practices—elementary harmonies, short solos framed by opening and closing ensembles, brass and saxophone sections that stated (sometimes in mild counterpoint) simple riffs, often written to be played in unison, and a clocklike four-four beat. Indeed, the riff became the identifying badge of the big band. The exception was Duke Ellington, whose music of the period still sounds almost avant-garde. Ellington, in fact, had begun replacing conventional big-band devices in the mid-thirties with new harmonies, his own brilliant melodies, and little concerto-type structures usually built around one soloist. These departures gave his band the sound of a unified instrument, rather than that of several determined platoons marching in the same general direction. Some of his inventions rubbed off in the mid-forties on such quixotic, short-lived organizations as those of Boyd Raeburn, Elliot Lawrence, Raymond Scott, and Billy Eckstine, while Stan Kenton was testing various independent approaches. Today, however, there are just four or five big jazz bands—Kenton, Gillespie, Basie, Ellington, and Herman—and they are, in the main, only heavier, more pompous versions of their earlier selves.

In the face of this melancholy situation, Columbia has released a new big-band record, "Miles Ahead: Miles Davis + 19," that is the most adventurous effort of its kind in a decade. All the ten selections, by a variety of hands, have been shaped by the gifted arranger Gil Evans into small concertos centered on Miles Davis, who plays the flügelhorn instead of the trumpet. Evans came into prominence in the early forties, when he wrote for the Claude Thornhill band a number of gliding, richly textured pieces that made use of such unorthodox instruments as the French horn. He reappeared as a collaborator with Davis and Gerry Mulligan in some of the suave, contrapuntal small-band recordings made for Capitol in 1949 and 1950. For "Miles Ahead," Evans' choice of instrumentation—five trumpets, three trombones, bass trombone, two French horns, tuba, alto saxophone, clarinet, bass clarinet, flute, bass, and drums—is an expansion of the ensemble involved in most of the Davis-Mulligan records. Plush, subtle sounds predominate, and the tempos, with two exceptions, are slow or medium. All the solos are by Davis, whose instrument sounds fogbound. Buried in all this port and velvet is Evans' revolutionary use, for such a large group, of structure, dynamics, and harmony. Reeds and woodwinds mix gracefully with the brass and then withdraw; trombones play countermelodies against sustained French-horn chords; a distant, undulating basso-profundo figure is part of the background for a stark Davis solo; another background figure, played in stop time, is repeated with slightly different harmonies and by slightly different combinations of instruments; trumpet shouts disappear abruptly into mutes. More important, Evans continually "improvises" on the melodies in the ensemble passages and rarely presents them anywhere in straightforward fashion. For all this, none of the pieces, except for parts of "Springsville" and "I Don't Wanna Be Kissed," ever get free from a chanting, hymnlike quality. There is, in fact, too much port and velvet, and Davis, a discreet, glancing performer, backslides in these surroundings into a moony, saccharine, and—in "My Ship"—downright dirgelike approach. The result is some of the coolest jazz ever uttered. (The use of the varying textures of other soloists might have relieved this.) Despite its technical innovations, "Miles Ahead" seems almost an epitaph for the cool school, whose beginnings are often dated by the Davis-Mulligan records and which has recently shown signs of wilting away. The playing throughout is impeccable.

Duke Ellington's newest record, "Such Sweet Thunder"

(Columbia), seems uncomfortably thin beside the work of Evans, who learned much from Ellington. The twelve numbers, all by Ellington and/or Billy Strayhorn, are supposedly based on incidents and characters in Shakespeare. Ellington says, puzzlingly, in the album notes about a tune called "Lady Mac," which begins in waltz time, "Though (Lady Macbeth) was a lady of noble birth, we suspect there was a little ragtime in her soul." "Lady Mac," "The Telecasters," "Up and Down, Up and Down," and "Half the Fun" are witty and lively pieces, but they are no more than casual sketches that depend largely on the soloists involved and not on the ensemble-solo development one expects from Ellington. The band, nevertheless, sounds almost as confident, precise, and full-bodied (in "Sister Kate," for example) as the great Ellington organization of 1940. It has few soloists the equal of Tricky Sam Nanton, Cootie Williams, Ben Webster, or Jimmy Blanton (Harry Carney and Johnny Hodges, though, are still on hand), but both Clark Terry and Quentin Jackson are not far behind.

February 1

MELEE

ONE OF THE DIFFICULTIES of describing an elusive music like jazz is a made-at-home terminology that includes such shapeless brand names as "swing," "bebop," and "Dixieland." The last of these, in particular, has recently developed as many meanings as those hopelessly splayed words "interesting" and "sophisticated." Fifteen years ago, "Dixieland" defined any small band made up of white musicians who depended on the sort of high-heeled collective improvisation performed around the time of World War I by the Original Dixieland Jazz Band. It didn't include "New Orleans" jazz, which was usually played by Negroes and was predominantly given over to complex crocheted ensembles, and didn't include "Chicago" jazz, which was originated in the late twenties by such men as Dave Tough, Jimmy McPartland, Bud Freeman, and Frank Teschemacher as a perfervid solo music that foreshadowed the swing era. Dixieland now embodies all these distinct types—or what is left of them—as well as the various new "revivalist" groups, which, to compound the confusion, are generally scarecrow imitations of such early New Orleans-style groups as those of King Oliver and Jelly Roll Morton. Nonetheless, at a concert titled "Dody in Dixieland," which was presented last Saturday night at eight-thirty and again at midnight in Carnegie Hall, the term was expanded still further, until, once and for all, it burst.

The forty-odd musicians who appeared on the program, which had all the confusion and blare of Coxey's Army, included a gospel singer, a bassist from the early days of bebop (Tommy Potter), half a dozen or so big swing-band musicians (Charlie Shavers, Tyree Glenn, Cozy Cole, and Roy Eldridge), some of the boys from the Chicago-style school (George Wettling, Jimmy McPartland, Bud Freeman), a Harlem stride pianist (Willie the Lion Smith), a couple of New Orleans-style musicians (Zutty Singleton and Tony Parenti), a vaudeville performer (John W. Bubbles), a trombonist who began in the twenties on the fringes of Dixieland but soon moved into a condensed, streamlined version of Chicago jazz (Miff Mole), and one Dixieland musician (the pianist Gene Schroeder). Three of the eight or so groups present had the look and instrumentation of Dixieland groups—those led by Stan Rubin, McPartland, and Wild Bill Davison—while the rest resembled everything from a chamber group to a Sousa band. There were motleys made up of three clarinets plus rhythm, five trumpets plus rhythm, and three trombones plus rhythm; a group composed of a vibraphonist, a bassist, and two drummers, one of whom sat in the dark off to one side of the stage and never touched his drums; and, at the opening of the second half of the concert, a swollen aggregation consisting of a pianist, two bassists, four drummers, and at least ten horns, which sounded like an overture to Armageddon. The only music of the evening occurred just after this display, when Bobby Hackett's flexible, highly imaginative six-piece group appeared and, after a nod in the direction of what has come to be a Dixieland standard, "Muskrat Ramble" (which was written by a New Orleans-style trombonist), performed three smooth, witty pieces that resembled the sound of the small Ellington groups of the forties and employed an almost endless variety of instruments, including cornet, tuba, bass saxophone, piano, baritone saxophone, tenor saxophone, alto trumpet, vibraphone, clarinet, and bass clarinet. Dody Goodman, an attractive comedienne who lent her name to the festivities, came onstage sporadically to trade quips with the m.c. ("I used to think the 'Jelly Roll Blues' was some kind of dessert"), did a brief soft-shoe routine with Mr. Bubbles that was announced as a "Cavalcade of the Dance," and throughout seemed as unnerved by the proceedings as everybody else.

February 8

VIC DICKENSON AND THE P.J.Q.

ONE OF THE GREAT jazz trombonists is Vic Dickenson, a lean, forty-nine-year-old, who in the past twenty years has perfected a combination of sly, prodding humor, graceful lyricism, and easy technical mastery that is unique on an instrument that has had very few able practitioners and that seems, like a faulty furnace, to devour the talents and energies of those who play it. Its career as a solo instrument has been comparatively brief. Until the big-band era of the early thirties, the trombone was largely either an ensemble instrument in small bands—in which, in a stertorous, down-in-the-cellar way, it filled in harmonic chinks—or, in the hands of men like Miff Mole and Kid Ory, a whiplash to keep things rolling. By the late thirties, however, it had become, with the help of Jimmy Harrison, J. C. Higginbotham, Dickie Wells, Jack Teagarden, and Dickenson, a first-rate, if erratic, solo vehicle. Only a handful of persuasive trombonists have turned up since (the difficult staccato mechanics of bebop and hard bop offer the trombonist technical problems that often make him sound like a fat man trying to run uphill), while of the older men only Teagarden, Benny Morton, and Dickenson have retained the push they started with.

A recent recording, "Vic's Boston Story" (Storyville Records), provides a generally satisfying demonstration of Dickenson's abilities. He is accompanied in the twelve selections by George Wein on piano, Jimmy Woode or Arvell Shaw on bass, and Buzzy Drootin on drums. Dickenson has a smooth, generous tone, and approaches a tune not as a full-dress improviser but as a funny and seemingly casual embellisher. Bleary, heavy-lidded glissandos appear side by side with stuttering triplets that often give way to swaggering, guttural sounds, full of a slapstick grace. In such slow numbers as "Yesterdays" and "All Too Soon," which he plays with and without a mute, his lissome near-whisper matches the celebrated chromium utterances of the late Tommy Dorsey, but it also has a smoky blue air that Dorsey never captured. In such up-tempo selections as "Lover Come Back to Me," his smears and snorts, occasionally broken by shouting phrases, bump out with an intense, unceasing rhythm. The more than ample solo space given Wein, a mediocre but sometimes rather moving pianist, unfortunately prevents Dickenson from ever really stretching his legs, as he did, say, in a Commodore recording made in the mid-forties called "Bottom Blues," on which he constructed two slow-tempo choruses—a mixture of groans, subterranean asides, and stately motion—that remain indestructible.

Dickenson is in excellent form on another recent record, "Buckin' the Blues" (Vanguard), performed by a group led by Buck Clayton and including Earl Warren on alto saxophone, Kenny Burrell on guitar, Aaron Bell on bass, Hank Jones, and Jo Jones. Most of the eight numbers are extended treatments of the blues and are built around Clayton, who plays with a gentle, garrulous lyricism—quick, glancing phrases, sustained blue notes, and a delicate, nervous vibrato. The rhythm section, with the exception of Hank Jones, a precise, nimble performer, tends to lumber, but Dickenson compensates for this by acting as a springy foil for the lighter-than-air ruminations of Clayton.

A recently formed group made up of vibraphone, piano, bass, and drums provides on its first release, "The Prestige Jazz Quartet" (Prestige), a refreshing contrast to the Modern Jazz Quartet, which has the same instrumentation and which shows signs of becoming fixed in a state of frozen fragility. The P.J.Q.—Teddy Charles, Mal Waldron, Addison Farmer, and Jerry Segal—plays with as much subtlety and intramural support as the M.J.Q., but, unlike the M.J.Q., which often submerges its content in spidery, complex forms borrowed from classical music, it handles its materials with a brisk expressiveness that makes secondary whatever forms are being used. Almost half of the recording is occupied by "Take Three Parts Jazz," an accomplished work by Charles. The piece, built around a couple of simple, appealing themes (one of them used as the basic idea for both the opening and closing parts), is actually a study of rhythms. Part 1 jockeys between an out-of-rhythm section and a brief fast section before settling into a pleasant medium tempo. Part 2 is a slow, romantic movement that slips in and out of tempo, and the final part is performed at a sturdy, flying tempo, ending in a delicate but hammering climax. The three other selections are of nearly equal interest—two adept numbers by Waldron ("Meta-Waltz" which moves back and forth between waltz and four-four time, and "Dear Elaine," a slow, deliberate ballad number), and a Thelonious Monk tune, "Friday the Thirteenth," which sets up an uncluttered platform for the soloists. Charles is a subdued, almost droning performer whose playing sometimes suggests the click of knitting needles and whose total lack of accent demands the listener's complete attention. Waldron offers a relaxed intensity that is full of rhythmic variations; series of elementary, highly melodic phrases are examined again and again, each time in slightly altered rhythmic patterns that generally build toward powerful climaxes (clusters of clean, ringing high notes in "Dear Elaine," and a long run of woodpecker notes in "Friday the Thirteenth").

Waldron and Charles appear in another recording, "Olio" (Prestige), a thoughtful effort that reveals the methodical control of Charles, who directed the session as well as contributed two of the six numbers. (Two are by Waldron, one is a standard, one is a blues.) Also on hand are Thad Jones on trumpet, Frank Wess on flute and tenor saxophone, Doug Watkins on bass, and Elvin Jones on drums. Thad Jones is a brassy, sure-footed trumpeter whose solos are now and then so perfectly structured they appear to have been carefully written out beforehand, and Wess, in contrast to the hardpan approach of most contemporary flutists and tenor saxophonists, achieves a soft and purposeful eloquence. Waldron's solos again attain a direct poignance that is indelible.

February 22

MONK

THE VINEGARY, dissonant, Gothic music that Thelonious Monk has been producing since his arrival, fifteen years ago, as a pianist and composer appears to be far more eccentric and difficult than the work of the other stubborn innovators, such as Jimmy Giuffre, Charlie Parker, and Charlie Mingus. Yet Monk, like these men, has been steadily reshaping, rather than rejecting, the traditions that preceded him. His playing, though camouflaged by the occasional use of an elbow and by dodging, jabbing rhythms, still reveals a stride pianist not at all dissimilar to two other former stride men, Duke Ellington and Count Basie. His compositions—with their bristling discords, unexpected notes, and impenetrable titles ("Crepuscule with Nellie," "Epistrophy") —are often no more than old blues, harmonically remodeled and infused with the shouting qualities of gospel music, a combination that conceals, beneath an armadillo exterior, a melodic sense easily as original and lyric as Ellington's. A diffident, evasive performer, whose feet sometimes flap about like fish while he plays, Monk invariably manages either to thoroughly imbue his coworkers with his rambunctious iconoclasm or, once in a while, to make them as awkward as wallflowers at their first dance.

Monk, who is now thirty-seven, came into prominence

when, along with Parker, Dizzy Gillespie, Charlie Christian, and Kenny Clarke, he helped found bebop. His playing has not changed appreciably since then. His runs are apt to sound stringy and higgledy-piggledy, his chords as if they were compounded of wrong notes. His touch always seems startled; scurrying, barely struck notes alternate with sudden, heavy chords that surprise the listeners as sharply as a thump on the back. But this apparent disarray is held together by its unfailing consistency, which, in turn, is dictated by an extraordinary rhythmic sense. If Monk plays a raggedy run, it is usually because he is trying either to retard the rhythm (sometimes this antic is simply an unabashed breathing space), or, if a banging discord comes next, to lift the rhythm, to force his colleagues to get up and go. The result is a superb unpredictability that has been shared by very few jazz improvisers. Monk's composing is less disordered. Although his songs ripple with dissonances and rhythms that often give one the sensation of missing the bottom step in the dark, they are generally written in simple riff figures that rarely stray from the accepted chorus structures. The best of them display minor, brooding melodies that, in their most intense moments, are peculiarly and delightfully reminiscent of pure, unsentimental lullabies.

Monk is in matchless form in four recent recordings—"Monk's Music: Thelonious Monk Septet" (Riverside), "Sonny Rollins" (Blue Note), "Mulligan Meets Monk" (Riverside), and "Thelonious Himself" (Riverside). In the first of these, Monk is joined by Ray Copeland on trumpet, Gigi Gryce on alto saxophone, Coleman Hawkins, John Coltrane, Wilbur Ware on bass, and Art Blakey. The six numbers—five by Monk, and one a nineteenth-century hymn—reflect the familiar prickly-pear Monk, as well as a remarkable, and heretofore largely undemonstrated, talent as an arranger. His scores for seven instruments have the depth and swagger that might be expected of a seventeen-piece group. The saxophones may work in unison for a few bars in the ensemble and then suddenly dissolve into counterpoint, while Monk plays a separate melodic line in company with the trumpet. This is abruptly broken by a series of harsh piano chords rhythmically and harmonically counter to everything else that is going on. The total effect, perfectly exemplified by "Well, You Needn't," is of a booming, controlled unsteadiness (the horns now and then sound like recruits attempting to fall in) that gives the impression—in contrast to the mannered ensemble writing in so much modern jazz—of being composed as it is played.

The first number, the hymn "Abide with Me," is played by the four horns in a pleasant, rasping, barbershop-quartet style. They deliver just a single chorus and—when one is prepared for the entrance of the rhythm section and the first solo—simply stop. It is unbearably tantalizing. "Well, You Needn't," "Off Minor," and "Epistrophy" are long, fervent, medium-tempo jumping exercises set in the conventional ensemble-solo-ensemble framework, and include satisfactory solos from everyone, despite the occasional scuffling brought about in "Epistrophy" by two players trying to start their solos at once. "Ruby, My Dear," one of Monk's casual but inimitable ballads, is divided up between his piano and Hawkins, who, as is his custom these days, manages, in both his fairly straightforward statements of the melody and his improvisations, to convert his materials into an impassioned music that seems almost visible. The final number, "Crepuscule with Nellie," is a slow, blues-like piece. The first half is played by Monk, with and without rhythm accompaniment; then the band enters to underscore the melody in such a way that it achieves an irresistible lullaby quality.

This mood occurs again on the record called "Sonny Rollins," during the performance of "Misterioso," a Monk tune, and one of the two numbers in which he appears. (There are six altogether.) This, played by, among others, Rollins, J. J. Johnson, and Art Blakey is a slow blues with a gentle, seesawing melody not unlike the traditional boogie-woogie walking bass. It results in a cradlelike motion that is perfectly offset by Rollins, who intones the most eloquent solo he has recorded.

"Mulligan Meets Monk" is an unsettling example of Monk as steamroller. On hand, in addition to Gerry Mulligan, are Ware and Shadow Wilson. Four of the six numbers are by Monk, one is by Mulligan, and one is a standard. Monk's playing is sprightlier than anything he has recorded in years, but Mulligan, an accomplished saxophonist, sounds as if he had just run a mile. His solos are crabbed and stilted; his ensemble work is uncertain and labored. The difficulty, perhaps, is the hopelessly different rhythmic approaches of the two men; Monk's is staccato, jumpy, sometimes almost arrhythmic, and Mulligan's is legato and flowing, in the manner of such cool practitioners as Miles Davis and Stan Getz. Some of the wreckage is cleared away by Ware, who, both in this case and in "Monk's Music," demonstrates an attack that is as startling as that of the late Jimmy Blanton. Although Ware often unfashionably plays his solos directly on the beat, they are now and then varied by graceful staccato or legato insertions, including meditative pauses and repetitions of a single note. These produce gliding, declarative melodic lines that, combined with a distinct yet soft tone, make a good many of his colleagues (who are apt to handle their instrument as if it were a horn) sound like riveters.

On "Thelonious Himself," Monk plays seven unaccompanied piano solos (he is joined in the eighth by Coltrane and Ware), three of them his own pieces and all of them in slow tempos that would be lackadaisical if it were not for the oblique, needling restlessness that invariably punctures the most aimless-seeming passage.

March 15

THIS WHISKEY IS LOVELY

RIVERSIDE RECORDS has reissued a unique and invaluable chunk of jazz archaeology, "Jelly Roll Morton: The Library of Congress Recordings" (Riverside), in twelve records, wherein Morton, the New Orleans pianist, arranger, and composer, reminisces, plays and sings several dozen songs, expounds his musical theories ("Vibrato . . . was nothing at the beginning but an imitation of a jackass hollering"), lies, brags ("I didn't name the 'Jelly Roll Blues' myself; it was named by the people of the city of Chicago"), and cavorts ("Oh, this whiskey is lovely") his way through some of the best performances he ever gave. The recordings, which are almost as legendary as Morton himself, were made for the Folk Music Division of the Library of Congress by Alan Lomax early in 1938, and they were a minor stroke of genius on his part, for Morton—old, tired, down-at-the-heels, and completely out of fashion—died just three years later. In the mid-forties, a limited edition of 78-r.p.m. recordings, a hodgepodge arrangement of most of what Lomax had taken down, was put on the market. It reappeared a few years later as a set of LP's, which soon went out of print. The present edition, which is pleasingly designed, includes an admirable fifteen-thousand-word essay on Morton by Martin Williams. At the same time, Riverside has inscrutably perpetuated many technical deficiencies in the recordings.

One is forced to battle the sharp gavel sound of Morton's shoe tapping out the beat, a volume that goes precipitously up and down, an endless series of squeaks, thumps, and rattles (the faulty equipment Lomax had to use), an unsteady recording speed that makes Morton's voice slide back and forth between a foghorn and an Irish tenor, and a system of collating that results, for example, in beginning the "Original Jelly Roll Blues" in Volume I and concluding it in Volume X. Fortunately, Morton was a forceful player and a clear speaker, and if one has decent sound equipment and does some athletic knob-twirling, nine-tenths of the material is intelligible.

Morton, a curious and appealing figure, was a highly talented Major Hoople. A handsome, intelligent, sensitive-faced man with an aquiline nose and a high forehead, he was born Ferdinand La Menthe of Creole parents in New Orleans around 1885, and by his mid-teens had become a proficient pianist, dandy, and gambler. He left the city for good about 1907, and for fifteen years roamed the country (he turned up in New York in 1911) as a vaudeville performer, gambler, patent-medicine man (Coca-Cola mixed with salt, at a dollar a bottle), cabaret owner, procurer, tailor, and occasional pianist and band leader. In time, he acquired a hundred and fifty suits, a diamond in a front tooth, and a diamond stickpin, watch, ring, and belt buckle, and he took to carrying a thousand-dollar bill. He also perfected a highly vocal vision of himself as a witty, adroit boulevardier. He became a full-time pianist, composer, and band leader in the early twenties in Chicago, and between 1926 and 1930 was responsible for some imperishable small-band recordings. (Inexplicably, only half-a-dozen reissues are now available, in Victor, Camden, Folkways, and Jazztone anthologies, but many of the old 78-r.p.m. discs are still around.) Then his luck ran out; he blamed a spell a West Indian had put on him. The early swing musicians considered him old-fashioned, jobs were infrequent, and he spent most of his last years as manager of a shabby night club in Washington, D.C.

Morton ranks with Louis Armstrong, Duke Ellington, and Charlie Parker as a great jazz innovator. His best small-band records are buoyant, fresh, and ingenious works full of revolutionary devices that are only now being rediscovered by modern musicians. Although they have all of the roomy, swaggering quality of spontaneous New Orleans jazz, they were, with the exception of the solos, largely written out. Each horn in the invariably rampaging final ensembles loosely follows a brilliantly sketched-out melodic line, in the fashion of the semi-arranged polyphonic exercises in Gerry Mulligan's recent sextet recordings. Such devices as the following gave structure, clarity, and variety to a music that was often accidental: three clarinets delivering a soft, engaging riff in unison against a trombone counter-melody; an orchestral passage led by a tuba, and another played without rhythm accompaniment (a recent "discovery" of the West Coast school of jazz); a Basielike rhythm-section passage that is started off by a booming trombone figure; a continual web of counter rhythms; graceful and extended melodic lines; and an uncommon attention to instrumental timbres and orchestral textures. Morton wrote easily a hundred compositions, many of whose titles have an eccentric motion of their own—"Tanktown Bump," "Pep," "Boogaboo," "Fickle Fay Creep." In contrast to the thirty-two-bar structure that became a confining fixture in the swing era, most of Morton's pieces were constructed, in the manner of ragtime, of carefully complementary parts of varying length. His melodies lack the subtle languor of Ellington's, but they have a solid, straightforward lyricism that is just as attractive. Today, Morton's piano often sounds romantic and old fashioned, and it is difficult to say why. It is true that his touch was undistinguished, that he used a lot of overweight, blurred chords in the right hand, and that his rhythmic approach tended toward the heavy ump-cha. Not only that, he favored rich, sweet, melodic figures that at times become downright lacy. Nonetheless, he was an accomplished technician whose left hand could slip deftly back and forth between intricate counter-rhythms and whose right could reel off arpeggios that compare favorably with those of Art Tatum. Beneath the predominantly decorative air of his style—even at fast tempos he seems to be bowing to the right and left—one finds complex, inspired, and thoughtful variations that match anything of their sort in jazz.

Half of the Library of Congress recordings are given over to talk, most of which is the core of *Mister Jelly Roll*, Lomax's book about Morton. Morton's soft, clear voice and easy rhythmic manner of speech are an unfailing pleasure. He was a magnificent tale-spinner who could make a New Orleans funeral or Memphis barroom brawl unforgettable. The rest of the recordings are a compact history of all the ingredients that went into the creation of jazz. Morton had a wonderful memory, and he effortlessly resurrects quadrilles, tangos, marches, spirituals, blues, boogie-woogie, stomps, rags, jazzed-up bits of opera, and an Indian Mardi Gras song. He even does some first-rate takeoffs, including a subtle and mischievous one on the blues, one on a popular song of the period (which he sings in a way that is strikingly like the whispers of Gene Austin and Rudy Vallée), and a delightful one on a bad honky-tonk pianist. Morton sang on only a handful of other records, which is a pity, for he belongs with Bessie Smith and Louis Armstrong as a jazz singer. His light, perfectly controlled baritone reveals a direct emotion that, in the half-dozen blues in these albums, results in some of the most affecting jazz vocals ever recorded. And, with few exceptions, he surpasses himself at the piano. "Creepy Feeling," one of his own pieces, which lasts eight minutes and is played at a slow tango tempo, is a hypnotic series of variations, each a development of the last. It is a remarkable performance. But it has, like much of the other music in the albums, a sad, ruminative quality, too. The bragging, spirited front of talk, talk, talk that sustained Morton suddenly makes perfect sense.

March 22

CLOSE, BUT NO CIGAR

ALTHOUGH JAZZ BEGAN as a vocal music, it has, peculiarly, produced only a handful of full-fledged jazz singers. There have been countless blues singers, ranging from the small, distinguished army of mud-voiced minstrels, like Blind Lemon Jefferson, who once roamed the South, to such clear-toned men as Jimmy Rushing and Joe Turner. But the blues singer is a highly specialized bird, whose technique, which is generally as primitive as his materials, rarely allows him to handle any other type of song. (Even Rushing is apt to sound as if he were trying opera in a tune like "Blue Skies.") There have also been innumerable "popular" singers who have been mistaken for jazz singers—Maxine Sullivan, Sarah Vaughan, Billy Eckstine, and Anita O'Day are some of them—largely because they tint their work with embellishments, blue notes, or husky tonal qualities. But these singers are, like outright popular singers, only the offspring of the Irish tenors and Victor Herbert sopranos who flourished forty years ago. The genuine jazz singer, who remains more of a vision than a reality, avoids sentimentality and, within the limitations of the human voice, parallels the timbres, rhythms, accents, and emotions achieved by the good jazz instrumentalist. The songs he sings, which can be limitless, serve only as casual frameworks for his ruminations. Louis

Armstrong is a matchless example. Lately his voice has bogged down in calculated grunts and rumbles, but he has created improvisations whose lyric invention equals anything he has done on the trumpet. The Billie Holiday of the late thirties and early forties is not far behind; the commonplace original melody of, say, "What a Little Moonlight Can Do," was long ago replaced by her recorded refashioning of it. Bessie Smith was a blues singer, but she used her dark, heavy voice with a majesty that transformed the blues into unique, brooding jazz singing, much as Mahalia Jackson converts an ordinary gospel song into an inspiriting kind of jazz. There have been lesser jazz singers, including Leo Watson, a demonic scat singer, who made a tune like "Jingle Bells" a boiling, incomprehensible incantation about snowbirds and big bass drums; Leadbelly; Julia Lee, a poignant, large-voiced Kansas City singer; Jack Teagarden, whose voice has a cool, seamless sound; Jelly Roll Morton, who sang with a genteel, yearning melancholy; Hot Lips Page; and Red Allen, a smooth offshoot of the young Armstrong. No new ones—with the exception of a few satisfactory blues singers, a couple of gospel singers, and a variety of bop-style scat singers, who sound like tobacco auctioneers—have appeared during the past fifteen years; indeed, the secret of jazz singing seems to have been lost.

These gloomy thoughts have been provoked by a new album, "Ella Fitzgerald Sings the Duke Ellington Song Book" (Verve Records), in which Miss Fitzgerald, in the space of four records, sings, scats, hums, and noodles her way through thirty-seven Ellington or Ellington-associated tunes. She is accompanied by his band in eighteen numbers and by two small groups in the rest; she does not sing in the album's "Portrait of Ella Fitzgerald," a new Ellington work in four movements. The album, done in soupy greens, browns, and oranges that leak disconcertingly over into the photographs (Miss Fitzgerald, a washed-out orange, leaning pensively on her elbow), includes lengthy biographical notes by Leonard Feather, written in a fervent sideshow manner ("this dignified, handsome, lusty, euphoric figure [Ellington], gliding through life as one on a throne with pneumatic wheels"). When Miss Fitzgerald, who is thirty-nine, got started as a jazz singer, in the mid-thirties, with Chick Webb, she had a thin, piping, highly rhythmic voice. Since then, it has gradually broadened into a deep contralto, and she has developed a technique that enables her to slide effortlessly up and down the scales, manage large intervals, and maintain perfect pitch. At the same time, her voice has taken on a soft edge that often blots out whatever jazz expression it once had. All the mannerisms of the jazz singer are there—an intensely rhythmic delivery, plenty of embellishment, and unfailing drive and enthusiasm—but they are only an extremely skillful overlay that invariably leaves her materials unchanged. She is a peerless popular singer.

The results, in the "Duke Ellington Song Book," are puzzling. Ellington is primarily a jazz composer who has become a songwriter by accident;: many of the tunes in the album were written as exercises for specific Ellington sidemen, and the lyrics were added later. The union has never seemed comfortable, for the lyrics, which are often inconsequential, tend only to get in the way of thoroughly self-sufficient compositions. (Ellington's out-and-out popular songs, on the other hand, have seldom been distinguished.) Nonetheless, Miss Fitzgerald is in perfect form, and she manages—particularly when she restricts herself to straightforward humming or scat singing—to point up just about all of the beauties at hand. Since her voice needs only skeletal accompaniment, the best moments in the album occur with the small groups, which include Ben Webster, Stuff Smith on violin, Oscar Peterson, and Barney Kessel or Herb Ellis. She rolls easily through "Do Nothing Till You Hear from Me," "Just A-Sittin' and A-Rockin'," the witty blues called "Rocks in My Bed," "Satin Doll" (which she hums and scats), and "Just Squeeze Me," an irresistible tune, which gets the most satisfying treatment in the set. Webster, whose rich tone and agile, affecting style are an ideal complement to Miss Fitzgerald's cushioned voice, hasn't played as well on recordings in a decade. It is Webster, in fact, who keeps the Ellington flavor intact. The big-band accompaniments are generally desultory. The band sounds heavy and indecisive, possibly because Sam Woodyard persists in a slogging, ticking afterbeat that becomes hypnotic. On the whole, Miss Fitzgerald sounds buried, but there are brief exceptions. She makes "I'm Just a Lucky So-and-So" into a hearty blues, and her second chorus in "Everything but You" is full of soaring variations that come close to pure jazz singing. Despite the red-carpet titles of the movements of "Portrait of Ella Fitzgerald"—"Royal Ancestry," "All Heart," "Beyond Category," and "Total Jazz"—the piece, described as a "suite," is little more than three mediocre tunes and a blues, all of them patched together by solos and by spoken introductions, which are delivered by Ellington and Billy Strayhorn in their best lemon-verbena fashion:

As the inspection of our royal subject gains momentum, we imagine we have been granted a confidential glimpse into her diary, and the more we leaf through the pages the more we realize that this *is* a personality of wonderful warmth, that she is all heart.

In the blues number, Clark Terry delivers two choruses which maintain an intensity that sounds very much like a man trying to blow his way out of what amounts to a paper bag.

April 5

OUT OF FOCUS

DURING THE PAST twenty years, the movies, radio, and television, together with short-story writers, novelists, and poets, have, with few exceptions, created an image of jazz as a loud, flamboyant, and rather foolish music. At the same time, a good many of its serious admirers have worked up a picture of it as a solemn, esoteric form that requires a degree in musicology to be understood. Both sides of this coin were plainly in evidence this past month in a couple of hour-long television programs—"The Timex All-Star Jazz Show," given last week over C.B.S., and "Swing into Spring," shown early in April over N.B.C.—and the first five programs, each half an hour, of a thirteen-week educational-television series, "The Subject Is Jazz," which is shown in New York by N.B.C. on Saturday afternoons.

The Timex show began with Garry Moore, its master of ceremonies, marching a group called the Dukes of Dixieland from the sidewalk into the studio. There Lionel Hampton's band took over by scrambling unsteadily through a fast number while Hampton beat on a tom-tom, threw his sticks up in the air, and then jumped on top of the drum and danced. The show ended, in an equally perspiring manner, with one of the strangest stews ever put together, which started with a series of solos in a medium-tempo blues by George Shearing, Gerry Mulligan, and Jack Teagarden. The tempo was suddenly hiked up, destroying a persuasive mood and paving the way for a singer named Jaye P. Morgan, who did a duet of "St. Louis Blues" with Louis Armstrong. They gave way to a short, clattering drum battle between Gene Krupa and Cozy Cole, at a still faster tempo, which led into some riffs by the Hampton band, during which Mr. Moore, who had been identified earlier in the show as an amateur drummer, used the wire brushes on a snare drum set up behind a music stand inscrutably labeled, "John Philip Sousa." The rest of the show was almost as febrile. Armstrong's small band delivered renditions of "Muskrat Ramble" and "Sunny Side of the Street" that matched, practically note for note, its earlier versions of those tunes. Shearing's quintet did a Cuban number and one chorus of "September in the Rain," which was taken up by the Dukes of Dixieland, a ragged, windy group which plays a music that bears as much resemblance to Dixieland as the fandango does. Miss Morgan sang two numbers, accompanied by Krupa, Chubby Jackson (bass), and a pianist, in an off-pitch voice that grew rapidly thinner and more quavery, until it seemed it might vanish altogether. Then, for three brief numbers, the music got on its feet, before subsiding into the finale. Teagarden appeared with a group that included Ruby Braff, Tony Parenti, Marty Napoleon (piano), Jackson, and Cole, and sang "Basin Street Blues" before being joined in "Jeepers Creepers" by Armstrong for a pleasant duet that was, however, stretched all out of shape by Armstrong's rubbery mugging. The Gerry Mulligan Quartet (Art Farmer, Henry Grimes, bass, and Dave Bailey) played a short, medium-tempo selection involving a superior solo by Farmer, who demonstrated, for the first and only time that evening, that spontaneity is part of jazz.

"Swing into Spring," which was built around Benny Goodman's present big band, was a stiff, fumbling attempt to recapture the days in the late thirties when Goodman was at the height of his popularity. The band, which had a stifled, clumping sound, in spite of such unidentified but recognizable men as Zoot Sims, Urbie Green, and Billy Butterfield (trumpet), did half a dozen numbers, among them the "Kink Porter Stomp," that involved some squeaking, fluttering trumpet work by Harry James. A small group, including Goodman, Teddy Wilson, and Red Norvo, puffed through a medley and accompanied Ella Fitzgerald and Jo Stafford, who alternated on such tunes as "I Gotta Right to Sing the Blues," "Hard-Hearted Hannah," and "How Come You Do Me Like You Do," and then collaborated on "St. Louis Blues." Ralph Burns, the composer, arranger, and pianist, conducted the Goodman band, augmented by fiddles and woodwinds, in a swooshing number of his own called "Spring Rhapsody." The McGuire Sisters, a vocal trio, bared their teeth and sang a couple of songs, and, for the final number, Goodman sang "It's Gotta Be This or That" in a firm, deliberate monotone.

The first few programs of "The Subject Is Jazz," with which the Educational Television and Radio Center, in Ann Arbor, Michigan, is concerned, consisted largely of some unenlightening mumbling between Gilbert Seldes, the host of the program, Duke Ellington, Billy Taylor, and Marshall Stearns, on such subjects as "What Is Jazz?," "Improvisation," and "Ragtime." In between, a group including such men as Tony Scott (clarinet, and tenor and baritone saxophones), Jimmy Cleveland, Taylor, and Osie Johnson performed dispirited samples. The fifth program, however, which delved into the subject of swing, was generally first-rate. There was some lucid discussion between Mr. Seldes and John Hammond, a highly knowledgeable jazz impresario, which was illustrated by a thirteen-piece group that included Buck Clayton, Benny Morton, Cleveland, Ben Webster, Paul Quinichette, Ed Thigpen, and Taylor. They played "For Dancers Only," using the Sy Oliver arrangement done for Jimmie Lunceford, the Fletcher Henderson arrangement of "King Porter Stomp," and Clayton's arrangement of "One O'Clock Jump," and a small group made up of the rhythm section and Clayton, Webster, and Morton sailed through "Flyin' Home." Clayton and Webster were in excellent form throughout, while Morton, particularly in "Flyin' Home" and "One O'Clock Jump," was impeccable. Perhaps the best moment in the show, as well as in the series to date, came during the sign off, when Webster could be heard in a solo that explained, in a matter of seconds, exactly what jazz is.

May 10

CHAMELEON

ALMOST EVERYTHING ABOUT Miles Davis, the trumpeter, seems ambiguous. A short, thin, retiring man, now thirty-one years old, who often stands motionless and slightly hunched when he plays, his horn pointed directly at the floor, like a crane poised on an unpromising mud flat, he is generally considered a founder of cool jazz, but his associates invariably includc some of the most perfervid members of the hard-bop movement. His playing sounds predominantly sweet and restrained, yet it conceals, much of the time, the basic hotness of men like Louis Armstrong and Roy Eldridge. Davis' debut, some twelve years ago, with such musicians as Charlie Parker and Max Roach, was wobbly. His approach consisted largely of an awkward blotting up of the work of Dizzy Gillespie. He had a shrill, mousy tone, he bungled more notes than not, and he always sounded as if he were playing in a monotone. Since then, his technique has improved steadily; his style, in fact, now comes in several shades. In slow numbers, he often uses a tight, resonant mute and, by playing directly into a microphone, achieves a hollow but penetrating sound, like blowing into the neck of an empty bottle. At the same time, he employs economical, melodic phrases spattered with a good many off notes, which give the effect of his casually twisting the melody—as if it were soft metal—into lumpy, yet graceful, shapes. Davis frequently plays open horn in middle tempos, and the change is startling. Although his tone is still slightly sour, series of fat, delicate phrases seem to round it off. They are reminiscent of a man slowly and rhythmically beating a soft punching bag. Fast numbers appear to unsettle him, for he often relies on a fretwork of empty runs and unsteady spurts into the upper register. But in a medium-tempo blues, say, Davis is capable of creating a pushing, middle-of-the-road lyricism that is a remarkable distillation, rather than a one-two-three outlining of the melodic possibilities; indeed, what comes out of his horn miraculously seems the result of the instantaneous editing of a far more diffuse melodic line being carried on in his head.

Two recent releases—"Relaxin' with the Miles Davis Quintet" and "Bags' Groove: Miles Davis and the Modern Jazz Giants" (Prestige)—give a complete picture of Davis' virtues and faults. In the first, which was made not long ago and is the less satisfactory of the two, he appears with John Coltrane, Red Garland, Paul Chambers, and Philly Joe Jones. There are six numbers, four of them standard tunes and one apiece by Dizzy Gillespie and Sonny Rollins. Davis uses a mute in five of them. The materials seem almost to be shrugged off; there are occasional sketchy ensemble figures, but, more often, only a string of rather haphazard solos. The most impressive moments occur in "If I Were a Bell," played at a pleasant up-tempo, and "Oleo," done slightly faster, in which Davis gets a balsa quality by using just bass accompaniment, except in the bridge, during which the rest of the rhythm section comes gallumphing in. Garland, a bright, dandyish pianist, also takes a surprisingly incisive solo in the lower register. "You're My Everything," which is slow-paced, is an excellent example of Davis the bottle blower; "Woody 'n' You," delivered at a fast clip, displays his nervous, squeaky style.

Coltrane, a student of Sonny Rollins, has a dry, unplaned tone that sets Davis off, like a rough mounting for a fine stone, while Jones, who has often performed as if he were singlehandedly drumming out an entire regiment, behaves throughout with restraint and sensitivity.

"Bags' Groove," on the other hand, contains some of Davis' most inspired work. The first side is given over to two versions of the title piece, a medium-tempo blues recorded late in 1954 with Milt Jackson, Thelonious Monk, Percy Heath, and Kenny Clarke. In both versions, Davis' solos, which are played open horn, have an oblique relentlessness and are full of neat, perfectly executed variations. Monk is superb. In the first version, his solo is broken by such long pauses that it appears he has left the studio; then he suddenly resumes, with clumps of clattering, offbeat dissonances. In the second version, his pressure up, he engages in a dizzy series of jagged runs. The rhythm section, in the manner of the old Basie rhythm section, which first put wheels on all the beats in the bar, moves without a bump. The second side has further clean, certain Davis, along with Rollins, Horace Silver, Heath, and Clarke. This is an indispensable record.

Vanguard has reissued two other indispensable efforts —"The Vic Dickenson Showcase," in two volumes, and "Buck Meets Ruby," made four years ago. These include some classic examples of an arbitrary type of small-band jazz that flourished between 1935 and 1945, and generally consisted of simple arrangements or improvised ensembles —the New Orleans type of ensemble, but with its tangles and intensities laid aside—built around the soloists. The musicians involved were, more often than not, members of the big bands of Fletcher Henderson, Cab Calloway, Count Basie, Duke Ellington, Benny Goodman, and so on. Temporarily freed of the strictures of their parent organizations, they usually reacted as if on holiday. Many of their records—particularly the Lionel Hampton Victors, the Teddy Wilson-Billie Holiday collaborations, the ones by the small Ellington units, and various Sidney Bechet "Feetwarmer" sessions—have an undying freshness. The Dickenson records Vanguard has reissued involve Ruby Braff; Shad Collins; Dickenson; Edmond Hall; Sir Charles Thompson, piano; Steve Jordan, guitar; Walter Page; and Les Erskine or Jo Jones. There are extended versions of ten standards and a couple of blues. Among them are strolling renditions of "Jeepers Creepers," "Russian Lullaby," and "I Cover the Waterfront" (which are, however, nearly flattened by the thump-thump-thump monotony of the Thompson-Page-Jordan-Erskine rhythm section), as well as slow, graceful interpretations of "Old Fashioned Love" and "When You and I Were Young, Maggie," which include some of Dickenson's finest work. "Old Fashioned Love" ends with a swaying, jostling ensemble in which Braff and Collins engage in slow-motion leapfrog, Hall slides discreetly around in the middle register, and Dickenson lays down a memorable floor of smears, growls, and rumbles. It is an enormously affecting example of collective improvisation.

"Buck Meets Ruby" concerns a group under the leadership of the pianist Mel Powell (Buck Clayton, Henderson Chambers, trombone, Jimmy Crawford, Hall, Jordan, and Page) and one under the leadership of Clayton (Braff, Buddy Tate, Benny Morton, Jimmy Jones, Jordan, Aaron Bell, bass, and Bobby Donaldson, drums). The Powell numbers (four, all standards) alternate between taut, jubilant ensembles and arranged passages, and they reach perfection in a long "I Must Have That Man," which, though played so slowly that it threatens to come to a dead stop, gradually develops a quiet, ascending lyricism that is extraordinary. Hall produces a sorrowing, practically trembling solo in the lower register that is unlike anything else he has recorded. The Clayton-Braff numbers (two standards and two originals) have a Basie sound, and there is notable work from everyone on hand. Clayton is a performer whose emotions are always on view, while Braff, a well-stirred mixture of Armstrong, Berigan, and Wild Bill Davison, plays with an almost overbearing legato attack that is frequently punctured by short connecting phrases and fleeting runs. The results are a dead heat.

May 17

THE M. J. Q. (*Continued*)

"MONTE KAY PRESENTS an Evening with the Modern Jazz Quartet," given a week or so ago at Town Hall, marked the first time that a jazz concert has been served up—greaseless and perfectly cooked—under glass. There were none of the Katzenjammer aspects of the usual jazz concert; in fact, the presentation was impeccable. John Lewis, the Quartet's leader, briefly described all the numbers, which (astonishingly) appeared in the order given in the program, which in turn expatiated on the selections in firm, no-nonsense terms ("'Angel Eyes,' by Matt Dennis. A lyrical American song popularized by Ella Fitzgerald"). The group, arranged in a neat semicircle on the stage, was dressed in tuxedos, and bowed in effortless unison to the applause. The concert, which was neither too long nor too short, was carefully worked out in both choice of materials and change of pace. Not a whistle or a catcall eddied the air. Indeed, the audience seemed to be steadily holding its breath, a band of bird watchers who had suddenly stumbled on an unknown species. Part of this general decorum was the result of the staging, and the rest was due to the Quartet, which, poker-faced and never fluffing a note or missing a beat, went at its instruments like jewelers intently at their work. After a time, one longed for a good sneeze or a rude shout to soften the atmosphere of unremitting industry.

The M.J.Q., which also includes Milt Jackson, Percy Heath, and Connie Kay, has made invaluable contributions to jazz in the four or five years of its existence. It has resuscitated, in quiet fashion, the art of collective improvising. It has reintroduced, through Lewis' compositions, the delicate, lyrical element of jazz (also present in the work of Jimmy Giuffre, Gerry Mulligan, and Charlie Mingus) that was stomped underfoot by the bop era. It has pointed the way toward the use of classical forms—the fugue, the rondo, and the episode—while maintaining, through some memorable improvisations and a frequent use of the blues, direct contact with the fundamentals of jazz. In the past year, however, the M.J.Q.—whether because of restlessness or too much conscientiousness—has tended to refine these approaches, with queer results. Many of the numbers it played at Town Hall seemed overboiled distillations of earlier versions of the same pieces. The solos, except for the ones by Jackson, who now and then played as if he might pop a button, were tentative and restrained, lest a loud noise or grinding chorus stain the materials at hand. In addition, the tonal qualities of the group appeared to rise higher and higher, as if from fright, until they became almost falsetto. Lewis stuck largely to the middle and upper registers, in both solos and accompaniment; Kay, a flawless if rather static performer, spent much of his time tiddling with his cymbals, which had a hard, high-pitched sound, or with a variety of tambourines, triangles, and finger cymbals (the few times he struck his snare drum, it sounded like thunder); and Jackson's vibraphone, an instrument that in the most skilled of hands has a light metallic timbre, was no more than a reflector for Lewis and Kay. This steady shrillness was particularly noticeable because of the absence of microphones, which made Heath's bass, which normally provides a respectable balance, barely audible.

There were seven pieces by Lewis, three by Charlie Parker, one by Dizzy Gillespie, and three standards. "Willow Weep for Me" was done as a solo by Jackson, who, though the best of the modern vibraphonists, revealed the limitations that always threaten his work. He does get a round, vibrating tone from his instrument (some vibraphonists sound as if they were rattling a bag of quarters), but at Town Hall he relied heavily on devices —a complex, staccato seesawing figure; the rapid hammering of a single note; a four-note phrase not unlike a traditional trumpet flourish—that after a while made every solo seem like a variation on the last one, instead of on a new melody. (Harry Edison, once a Basie trumpeter, has a good deal in common with Jackson in this respect.) Two examples of the M.J.Q. as distillers occurred in "Two Degrees East Three Degrees West" and "A Night in Tunisia." The first is a simple, charming blues by Lewis, yet the Quartet peeled off all the outer melodic wrappings, delivering in its ensembles a series of clandestine chords that only implied the melody. "A Night in Tunisia," whose repeated descending phrases build gradually to a breathtaking break and the entrance of the first soloist, received the same treatment. Moreover, the break was eliminated, and so was much of the excitement of the piece. The first half of the concert was closed by a flowing but tenuous fifteen-minute work by Lewis, "Fontessa" (described as "a little suite inspired by the Renaissance Comedia Dell'arte"), which involved a series of improvisations on three extremely pleasant themes in the form of a blues, a ballad, and a boplike number.

Four of the numbers in the second half were from a score by Lewis for a recent French motion picture, and though they consisted of such things as a triple fugue, funeral music, a blues, and some heated triangle work by Kay, they sounded much like "Fontessa." The rest were by Charlie Parker, and in them the Quartet finally began to loosen its galluses, an attitude that continued during the three encores, when it really got down to business by playing with a lightness and fervor that hid, for the first time that evening, its glistening techniques.

A doughy, fast-talking disc jockey named Art Ford is both master of ceremonies and producer of a new, no-holds-barred jazz program, "Art Ford's Jazz Party," which lasts no less than an hour and a half and can be seen Thursday evenings over WNTA. Most of the jazz on television in the past ten years has seemed to be piped from a museum or a vaudeville stage; Ford, who, in the first two shows, has said a great many things like "This is the kind of jazz you can't buy," and "Our switchboards are jammed with phone calls," in addition to talking about the genuine, no-rehearsal spontaneity, is apparently aiming toward the virgin forests between the two extremes. His talk has at least been more agile than the music, which, though surrounded by all the paraphernalia of somebody's back room at 3 A.M.—loosened ties, bottles, cigarette smoke, casual bystanders—fits easily into the vaudeville tradition.

On the first program, a band made up of, among others, Rex Stewart, Pee Wee Russell, Wilbur de Paris on trombone, Chuck Wayne on guitar, and Zutty Singleton elbowed its way through such pre-Boer War numbers as "Royal Garden Blues," "Basin Street Blues," and "Sweet Sue." Russell, who is now in the queer position of being at once a legend and a neglected musician, sounded defensive and forced in "Sugar," done as a solo, and Singleton, who has refined the use of the cowbell, wood block, and tom-tom into a set pattern that he never tires of, played, in his solo number, as if he were shifting a log pile. In between, a loud trombonist from Johnny Long's band was featured, as well as a young tenor saxophonist who very nearly played in tune. Josh White, presumably in the wrong studio, sang, and Stewart played a slow blues that began with great poignance and ended abruptly in a screech, just three choruses later. There was also a ten-minute sack race, "Honeysuckle Rose," which was described in the *Times* the next day as "unforgettable." The *Times* was right.

The second show was built around Stewart, Ben Webster, Miff Mole, Buster Bailey, and Johnny Guarnieri on piano, plus a guitar, a bass, a vibraphone, and drums. Although predominantly a swing group, they chose such numbers as "Basin Street Blues," "Muskrat Ramble," and "That's a Plenty," which had, largely because of Bailey's flat clarinet and Stewart's cleaverlike tone, a rather oriental flavor. Maxine Sullivan sang two songs well; an enormous blues shouter, Big Miller, confused the styles of Joe Turner and Joe Williams; and there were brief display numbers for Stewart, Webster (who growled almost continually, a smoke-screen device he disappears into when ill at ease), Bailey, and Mole, who, though sixty now, roared and swashbuckled along all evening like a ten-year-old. A welter of riffs, based on "St. Louis Blues," closed the program. Everyone was in shirt sleeves.

May 24

BEN WEBSTER

THE SAXOPHONE, an uneasy amalgam of the oboe, clarinet, and brass families invented a century ago by a Belgian named Adolphe Sax, has always seemed an unfinished instrument whose success depends wholly on the dexterity of its users. In the most inept hands, the trumpet, say, is always recognizable, while a beginner on the saxophone often produces an unearthly, unidentifiable braying. Even good saxophonists are apt to produce squeaks, soughs, honks, or flat, leathery tones. Thus, the few masters of the instrument—jazz musicians like Coleman Hawkins, Lester Young, Harry Carney, Hilton Jefferson, and Ben Webster (classical saxophonists usually play with a self-conscious sherbetlike tone)—deserve double praise. Ben Webster, the forty-nine-year-old tenor saxophonist from Kansas City, has for almost twenty years played with a subtle poignancy matched only by such men as Hawkins and Johnny Hodges (from both of whom he learned a good deal), Lucky Thompson, Herschel Evans, and Don Byas. A heavy, sedate man, with wide, boxlike shoulders, who holds his instrument stiffly in front of him, as if it were a figurehead, Webster played in various big bands before the four-year tour of duty with Duke Ellington that began in 1939. Since then, he has worked with small units and his style, which was developed during his stay with Ellington, has become increasingly purified and refined. Like the work of many sensitive jazz musicians, it varies a good deal according to tempo. In a slow ballad number, Webster's tone is soft and enormous, and he is apt to start his phrases with whooshing smears that give one the impression of being suddenly picked up by a breaker and carried smoothly to shore. Whereas Hawkins tends to reshape a ballad into endless, short, busy phrases, Webster employs long, serene figures that often (particularly in the blues, which he approaches much as he might a ballad) achieve a fluttering, keening quality—his wide vibrato frequently dissolves into echoing, ghost-like breaths—not unlike that of a cantor. His tone abruptly shrinks in middle tempos and, as if it were too bulky to carry at such a pace, becomes an oblique yet urgent and highly rhythmic whispering, like a steady breeze stirring leaves. In fast tempos a curious thing frequently happens. He will play one clean, rolling chorus and then—whether from uneasiness, excitement, or an attempt to express the inexpressible—adopt a sharp, growling tone that, used sparingly, can be extremely effective, or, if sustained for several choruses, takes on a grumpy, monotonous sound. At his best, though, Webster creates, out of an equal mixture of embellishment and improvisation, loose poetic melodies that have a generous air rare in jazz, which is capable of downright meanness.

Webster is in faultness condition in two recent recordings, "Bill Harris and Friends" (Fantasy) and "Gee, Baby, Ain't I Good to You: Harry Edison" (Verve). In the first, he is given as much space as Harris, a tufted-toned trombonist who delivers bunches of dogged, vibratoless notes that seem to perforate rather than transform the melody. The contrast to Webster's style is striking. There are seven numbers, all of them standards, including a spoofing of sweet music—"Just One More Chance"—that is more energetic than funny. (Jazz and slapstick rarely mix.) Webster gives a classic five-and-a-half-minute treatment to a slow ballad, "Where Are You?;" plays a memorable solo in "I Surrender, Dear," again at a slow tempo; and then in Ellington's "In a Mellotone," which is done at a relaxed jog and lasts almost ten minutes, puts together a long, perfectly sustained set of variations that are possibly the best he has ever recorded. The rhythm section (Jimmy Rowles on piano, Red Mitchell on bass, and Stan Levey on drums) is precise but timid. It brings to mind the handful of records Webster made in the mid-forties with Sidney Catlett, who brushed aside Webster's occasional tendency to coast by ceaselessly pushing him with sharp, perfectly timed rimshots and bass-drum beats. Webster has never played with quite the same intensity since.

On the second record, Webster appears with Harry Edison, Oscar Peterson, Barney Kessel, Ray Brown, and Alvin Stoller (drums). There are seven standards, including three extremely pleasant blues. Edison, a casual repetitive soloist, shares a good deal of space with Kessel and Peterson, who are intense but equally repetitive performers. The rhythm section, indeed, has a clogged, airless sound that seems to hobble Edison, if not Webster, who, particularly in the opening of his solo in "Taste on the Place," lines along as gracefully as a gull.

"Trav'lin' Light: The Jimmy Giuffre 3" (Atlantic), is a conscientious, peculiarly static series of embellishments on the techniques—intricate, partly written contrapuntal ensembles; short solos; the absence of a sounded beat—evident in Giuffre's one previous trio recording, which, even in its more mournful moments, had a buoyant, Pan-like quality. One reason for this deliberateness is a change in instrumentation; the bassist has been replaced by the valve trombonist, Bob Brookmeyer, whose work often resembles that of the late Brad Gowans. (Jim Hall, the guitarist, remains, and Giuffre, as usual, alternates between the clarinet and the tenor and baritone saxophones.) At the same time, the tonal qualities of Brookmeyer's instrument both fill in and blur the outlines of the original trio, which had a pleasant brittleness. Another reason is Giuffre's predominant use of ensembles—there are almost no solos—in which the three voices wind heavily around one another, like garrulous people gossiping away a hot summer evening. There is, however, excitement in such numbers as "Forty-second Street," "Show Me the Way to Go Home," and "The Swamp People" (there are, in all, four numbers by Giuffre and four standards), but it evaporates in the slow, lyrical pieces, in which Giuffre sticks to the clarinet, playing it in a pale, hesitant, gloved manner, as if he were trying to imply rather than state his music.

Some of this determined indirectness occurs again in "Jimmy Giuffre and His Music Men Play 'The Music Man' " (Atlantic). He has arranged eleven numbers from the current musical for four saxophones, three trumpets, a bass, and drums, and Meredith Willson's score, which is full of turn-of-the-century brass-band music and parlor songs, takes on a muted blues sound that suggests that Giuffre could probably make an entire symphony orchestra seem like his trio plaintively discoursing in a back room.

June 21

BIG SID

DECCA HAS REISSUED, on two LPs, "Louis Armstrong Jazz Classics" and "Satchmo's Collectors' Items," twenty-four records made by Armstrong with groups of various size, between 1935 and 1941 that are valuable not only for the presence of Armstrong—at the time, the taut directness of his earliest style had reappeared and become a kind of ballast for the Alpine lyricism he developed in the late twenties—but for the presence, on two-thirds of them, of Sidney (Big Sid) Catlett, the near-legendary drummer who, though he died seven years ago, is still an irreplaceable performer. The Decca collections are not altogether satisfactory. Instead of personnel and recording dates, we are given long, repetitive, parboiled accounts of Armstrong's career—a Horatio Alger tale that has been intoned so often it has taken on the air of a publicity release. Moreover, the selections appear to have been made blindfolded. Although Armstrong recorded well over a hundred numbers for Decca during the period, among them enough classic material for four superior LPs, the collections include much that is mediocre. Nonetheless, what comes plunging through, as firmly as Armstrong himself, is Catlett, who, by the time he joined Armstrong, in 1938, had perfected a unique and faultless style that began to go awry only when he became ill, in the late forties.

Catlett's career was a singularly queer one, even for jazz, whose history is filled with the wreckage of poverty, sudden obscurity, and premature death. Born in Evansville, Indiana, in 1910, he came into prominence in New York with, among others, the bands of Elmer Snowden (a remarkable kindergarten that included such other beginners as Roy Eldridge, Chu Berry, and Dickie Wells), Benny Carter, Fletcher Henderson, and, finally, Armstrong. He stayed with Armstrong until 1942, except for a brief period in 1941 with Benny Goodman, who, though Catlett contributed immeasurably to some of Goodman's most relaxed big-band efforts ("Pound Ridge," "The Count," "I Got It Bad and That Ain't Good"), abruptly let him go, reportedly because Catlett, a superb showman, was upstaging him. Then Catlett won a couple of magazine awards, and celebration seemed at hand. He worked in New York with a memorable Teddy Wilson group (Emmett Berry, Joe Thomas, or Bill Coleman on trumpet, Edmond Hall on clarinet, and Benny Morton on trombone), which was never recorded, and then with his own excellent quartet, which included Ben Webster and which made a handful of records now rarer than ambergris. In 1947, he rejoined Armstrong, who then had Earl Hines, Barney Bigard, and Jack Teagarden, a wonderfully limber band that was recorded during several concerts and whose recordings are still available from Victor and Decca. But it was a peculiar time for jazz. The music was quiescent during the war; a good many of the large number of jazz recordings made in the forties were done for obscure labels; and by 1946, the music itself was in a state of discombobulation, brought on by the slow disintegration of the swing era and the arrival of bebop. True to form,

Catlett died at the beginning of the most successful time jazz has ever known.

Coleman Hawkins is perhaps the only jazz musician, alive or dead, who approaches Catlett's extraordinary adaptability, for Catlett worked successfully with such disparate jazz musicians as Sidney Bechet, Eddie Condon, Hot Lips Page, Goodman, and Ellington, as well as Dizzy Gillespie and Charlie Parker on a couple of the fieriest bebop records ever made. His style appears to have been almost totally his own. (His use, particularly with Bechet and Armstrong, of several types of press roll, for both accompaniment and solos, suggests the early work of Zutty Singleton, and the way he employed the wire brushes and the high-hat and other cymbals is reminiscent of Chick Webb.) Its main characteristics were an intense, buoyant, metronomic beat (it is surprising how many good drummers cannot keep perfect time), which he would now and then hurry very slightly to give the effect of urgency; a light, forceful touch, a sensitivity to what was going on elsewhere in a group that sometimes uncannily resulted in the anticipation of what a soloist was about to do; a technique that was always sufficient for what he had in mind (as opposed to the remarkable technique of Buddy Rich, which has long existed for the sake of itself); and a consummate taste.

Catlett was an inspired accompanist. Always conscious of dynamics (a fundamental largely foreign to modern drummers), he would use a light, clear cymbal behind a clarinet solo; half-closed high-hat cymbals, which produce a heavier, treading-water effect, behind a trumpet; a Chinese cymbal (whose edges are perforated with holes through which naillike pieces of metal are loosely hung, making a sound exactly like water spattered on a hot griddle), or the full high-hat, played in a clipped, flowing manner, behind a trombone; a closed high-hat, which gives a ticking effect, like a rubber eraser being tapped on metal, behind a bass or piano. At the same time, Catlett's left hand would work out inimitable series of accents on the snare-drum head, on the head and rim simultaneously (a rimshot), or by hitting one stick, held firmly against the snare head, with the other, which resulted in a pleasantly thick chonking sound. Catlett's left-hand rhythms, indeed, had something in common with certain of Stravinsky's rhythmic practices; they were wholly unpredictable, yet always right, and they created a spare trampolinelike tension off which the most sluggish soloist tended to rebound. His work on the bass drum, which until then was used by most drummers to emulate the tread of a giant, alternated between soft but solid beats, complete pauses, and sudden offbeats, which paralleled the work of Jo Jones and foreshadowed the bop drummers. And his use of wire brushes (a rapidly vanishing art) varied between a rich, distinct padding sound at fast tempos and, at slower speeds, a crystalline sound, like fingernails on wood.

Most drum solos are wild fountains of noise. Catlett, like (occasionally) Jo Jones, Shelly Manne, Art Blakey, and (very occasionally) Buddy Rich, was an exception. He was, after Baby Dodds, the first of the melodic drummers. He might, in a five-minute excursion, begin (using the sticks) with a series of quiet, delicate, sharp figures on the snare head, release the snares (so that a tom-tom effect was produced), move rapidly between the head and the rims (tickety-*thump* tick-tack-tick-*thump-thump*), and then (switching to mallets) move over to the tom-toms, while gradually intensifying his patterns and volume. Then he would suddenly break the flow with a perfectly placed silence, move back to the snare drum (using sticks again), return to a whisper, and with the snares on once more, start working toward a crescendo, which generally would incorporate a series of abrupt, stunning explosions, carried out on every part of his set with a speed and definition that even Rich, who drums faster than light, has never matched. Catlett the showman often appeared in his solos. Well over six feet tall, with enormous shoulders and slender fingers the length of dinner knives, Catlett sat at his drums with Prussian erectness, his trunk motionless and his arms (weighted by hands that made drumsticks look like matches) moving so fast that they seemed to be lazily spinning in slow motion. It was an unforgettable ballet. Once in a while he would twirl his sticks over his head or throw them in the air, allowing their motions to silently measure off several beats. The effect was louder than any shout.

There are tantalizing glimpses of Catlett's work in the Decca reissues. Although the performing groups include such men as Red Allen, Wilbur de Paris, and J. C. Higginbotham, they are miserable organizations, with gluey, Lombardo saxophones, a precision in the various sections reminiscent of marching recruits, and desultory arrangements. It is Catlett and Armstrong, a couple of bookends, who prevent them from flying hopelessly apart. In the final choruses of "Bye and Bye," one can hear how Catlett, using tight, powerful rimshots on the afterbeat, could drive a big band to a climax. His left hand is in excellent evidence all through "Hear Me Talkin' to Ya" and

"Savoy Blues," in which he lays down a thick carpet of press rolls. Toward the end of "Save It Pretty Mama," he slips into a soft afterbeat behind Armstrong, subtly shifting the rhythm from an even glide to a slow, irresistible rock. In "You Rascal You," he ticks the snare-drum rims every four measures behind Armstrong's vocal, as though he were counting telegraph poles from a slow train—an invention used, in a slightly different fashion, by most modern drummers, and generally credited to Art Blakey. Perhaps the best example of Catlett's precision and excitement occurs in "Baby, Won't You Please Come Home," when he closes Higginbotham's trombone solo with an emphatic rimshot, followed by a pause, and, a split second after Armstrong's horn enters, another emphatic rimshot, which sends Armstrong rolling down the road. It's an electric moment.

June 28

MAMMOTH (*Continued*)

SINCE ITS BEGINNINGS, in 1954, the Newport Jazz Festival has, like a contented city dog, slowly grown sleeker and rounder. The first Festival consisted of two modest concerts attended by some fifteen thousand people. The latest Festival, held over the Fourth of July weekend in an endless arena called Freebody Park, was a statistician's dream: There were seven concerts (afternoon and evening) and two musically illustrated morning lectures, all of which amounted to over thirty-five solid hours of music and talk; approximately two hundred and fifty musicians, including five big bands, sixteen singers, and a welter of small groups; and a total attendance of sixty thousand. Indeed, the Festival now belongs in the same boat as the Empire State Building, the Grand Canyon, and Alaska. But bigness is more partial to flabbiness than muscle, and the bigger the Newport convention has grown, the softer it has got. Aside from such superficially discomfiting trivia—the sort of trivia that when multiplied can seem mountainous—as asking an audience tightly packed on wooden camp chairs to remain attentive for six hours at a time, introductory Capitol Hill remarks by Senator Green (R.I.), the public presentation to musicians of several awards by the magazine *Playboy*, the ceaseless churring of movie cameras that surrounded the bandstand, and a C.B.S. broadcast that, because of the demands of sponsored radio, got all the evening concerts off to a shambling, indeterminate start, there were such out-and-out misfires as an interminable Benny Goodman evening, in which Goodman, heading a dispirited, ragged big band, played nervously and off pitch; the International Youth Band, a theoretically heartening aggregation made up of eighteen of the leading players from sixteen nations, which, because of the largely pompous, choked arrangements it was forced through, sounded heavy and listless; a small modern group, including flute, oboe, tuba, timpani, xylophone, and vibraphone, that produced a half hour of tinkling, be-boom, and oompah; several enormous female singers, displacing nearly half a ton, who sang with a resolute, ringing monotony; the big Maynard Ferguson band, which whumped and squeaked like a frightened beaver; and an amorphous small group, made up of Urbie Green, Terry Gibbs (vibraphone), Dinah Washington, Don Elliott (mellophone and vibraphone), and Max Roach, that went on forever, particularly in a vibraphone duet, which after a time achieved an effect like coconuts raining on a tin roof.

The exceptions were almost extracurricular in nature. On Friday morning, during a garbled lecture by Professor S. I. Hayakawa, a semanticist from San Francisco State College, on "The Origin and Nature of the Blues," Jimmy Rushing, who provided the accompanying demonstrations, sang—backed by a six-piece Dixieland band, Eli's Chosen Six, which puffed itself blue behind him—eight numbers with an easy, shouting articulateness (he has a way of rounding off every word, like a man polishing an apple to a gleam) that, in such works as "Careless Love," "Goin' to Chicago," and "St. Louis Blues," he has rarely equaled.

On Saturday morning, Marshall Stearns gave an informed and amusing rundown on jazz dancing, which was illustrated with two dozen interludes by two remarkable dancers, Leon James and Al Minns, who seemed in motion even while standing stock-still, and who did the Cakewalk, the Shake Dance, the Camel Walk, the Eagle Rock, the Shimmy, the Charleston (seven variations), the Jig Walk, the Lindy Hop, Trucking, the Suzy-Q (the Arthur Murray version, as taught in 1936, and the legitimate version), the Shorty George, the Big Apple, and a good many more. During the Big Apple (1938), a dance with sixteen separate steps, Minns executed a section in exquisitely slow slow motion, moving his arms and legs in a series of spare swoops and wide steps, which sustained, for perhaps a minute, a liquid tension that was extraordinarily poignant and graceful. This was balanced by a dance called the Shag (1938), which consists of extremely fast, short steps, delivered while the dancer—stiff as a ramrod, his arms at a forty-five-degree angle over his head—moves directly up and down like a lightning pile driver, and by the Apple Jack (1945), a dance done to bebop by James, who gave the impression of creating a casual, contrapuntal offsetting melody. Minns and James closed the morning with a two-part sketch—a man asking a woman to dance in the days of the Big Apple and in the present time of cool music—that was a masterpiece of exact, funny, understated satire. And on Sunday morning, just after midnight, at the end of a long evening devoted to the blues and including a superior performance by the Gerry Mulligan Quartet, Mahalia Jackson, accompanied by a pianist, organist, and bass player, sang a dozen spirituals and gospel songs. Miss Jackson's presence on a stage is a hypnotic lesson in graciousness and poise, and this, combined with a rich alto voice that bends and slides around her materials like a wide, placid river, made her performance perfection, particularly in a soft, nearly tempoless rendition of the Lord's Prayer, which had an honesty and melodic delicacy that brought tears to the eyes.

There were other good things, which, like fireflies, winked steadily away in the general murk. On Thursday evening, Joe Morello, the drummer of the Dave Brubeck Quartet, displayed—in a long series of four-bar exchanges with his cohorts—a fresh, decisive imaginativeness, a sense of rhythm, and quick, shifting emphases that recalled some of the snap, pop, and crackle of Sidney Catlett. On the same night, Duke Ellington, in the course of fifteen numbers, a good many of them pleasant new compositions, again and again pushed his band until its unique unison-voiced textures and superb timing became, as they have in the past, one large, floating collective voice—a momentarily realized dream of what a big jazz band should be. On Friday afternoon, the Jimmy Giuffre 3, a group that hasn't been successfully recorded yet, performed five numbers, including a medium-tempo version of Giuffre's "That's the Way It Is." It was centered on a short blues-spiritual theme that was bandied about in brief solos and ensemble passages full of counterpoint, echoing fugal bits, and nicely jarring timbres. It was an irresistible performance. The next afternoon, Herb Pomeroy and his big band played half a dozen blazing Kentonish-Basielike arrangements and then—in its final number, "The Lunceford Touch," done in the manner of the Lunceford band—got off some brass figures that were so loud and so brilliantly executed that the air in the park seemed to be rolled right back to the bleachers. On Sunday afternoon, Thelonious Monk, accompanied by bass and drums, was, in an almost perversely quiet way, matchless. Sonny Rollins, who appeared just before (also with bass and drums), was allowed exactly two numbers (Anita O'Day, a good popular singer, was allowed seven selections earlier in the afternoon), but managed to suggest forcibly his skill at masterly improvisations compounded of fast runs, lazy, sway-backed melodic phrases, and jolting off-rhythms. Jimmy Knepper, the trombonist with a small group led by Tony Scott, who played with a fervency bordering on desperation, proved again that he is the first trombonist since J. J. Johnson with his own style—one that is a mixture of the directness of Benny Morton and the obliquity of Johnson. The Festival was closed that night by Louis Armstrong's small band (which includes, among others, Peanuts Hucko, Trummy Young, and Billy Kyle), whose past Newport performances have been mostly vaudeville in nature. There was still plenty of vaudeville in evidence—off-color jokes and words, facial contortions, and the like—but in at least half of his twenty numbers Armstrong played with a controlled, feverish lyricism (in such numbers as "Sunny Side of the Street," "Mack the Knife," and "The Star-Spangled Banner") that suddenly dispelled the chromium-and-tail-fins pall that had hung stubbornly over most of the weekend.

July 15

THE OLDEN DAYS (*Continued*)

ALMOST WITHOUT EXCEPTION, the second annual Great South Bay Jazz Festival, which consisted of five evening concerts, held in an open-sided sailing ship of a tent in Great River, Long Island, over the last weekend of July and the first of August, was, for a combination of who knows what reasons—fitful production, bad weather, the doldrums of a gray, wet summer, a general lack of musical inspiration—a desultory, aimless affair that made last year's Festival, which included extraordinarily sustained work by Coleman Hawkins, Yank Lawson, Jimmy Giuffre, and Charlie Mingus, seem a legendary event. This year, performance after performance turned out to be either uncooked or exasperatingly dull.

The South Bay Seven (with Rex Stewart, Benny Morton, and Jerome Richardson on flute and baritone saxophone), which opened the Festival, played eight numbers that alternated between vague, rather dumpy Ellingtonish selections and rackety free-for-alls (all of them weighed down by a spiritless rhythm section) that were briefly improved by Richardson, who, making his way vigorously upstream, contributed to a slow "Tin Roof Blues," a solo with a yearning, hallooing climax that was, in the circumstances, stunning. The following weekend, a quartet led by the baritone saxophonist Pepper Adams (Kenny Burrell was on guitar, George Duvivier on bass, and Elvin Jones on drums) did half a dozen numbers that went on and on in a heated monotone, like an enormous freight train. Adams has a curiously muffled, oblique tone, as if his notes evaporated when they hit open air, and he plays in the manner of the hard-boppers (fast, skidding runs, thick staccato phrases, and an almost indiscernible rhythm), who are apt to float around for twenty choruses whether they have something in mind or not. The Fletcher Henderson All-Stars (eighteen strong, and including Joe Thomas and Taft Jordan on trumpets, Morton, Dickie Wells, Hilton Jefferson, Buddy Tate, and Stewart as leader) played with a volume that was equaled only by its raggedness. The saxophones kept stepping on each other, the trumpet section wavered and bleated, and most of the rhythm section was inaudible beneath the slamming, abrasive drumming of Mousie Alexander, all of which converted a spacious and pleasant new work by Stewart and Dick Cary, called "Georgia Sketches," into a shambles.

On the final night of the Festival, Charlie Mingus, heading a group made up of Shafi Hadi on alto and tenor saxophones, Horace Parlan on piano, Jimmie Knepper, and Danny Richmond, worked his way through three superior numbers, which included a blues ingeniously hooked up to an extremely attractive melody, several rhythms, breaks, and some first-rate solos. (A fourth number was centered on an actor, Melvin Stewart, who, accompanied by Mingus on piano, read some bad poems.) And then, the pot on the lip of boiling, the group packed up and left. The evening was closed by Duke Ellington, who delivered a new four-part piece, "The Great South Bay Jazz Festival Suite," consisting of an Afro-Cuban number, a reshaping of "Rosetta," and a long blues in two sections. This had some flowing trombone figures pitted against the solo horn of Harry Carney, two excellent choruses of muted wah-wah trombone by Quentin Jackson, and a solo by Paul Gonsalves. Gonsalves, like Pepper Adams, got caught in his own momentum, but he was eventually carried along by the band, which began developing, with a series of arch, tight brass figures, an irresistible rocking motion, and then, just as the tent seemed about to be puffed away, stopped. For the next dozen numbers, Ellington fell back on such things as an absurd Spanish pirouette featuring the trumpet of Cat Anderson, who squeaked mightily; a couple of numbers from his "A Drum Is a Woman"; a number called "Hi Fi Fo Fum" and built around an interminable tom-tom solo by Sam Woodward (who handled every number as if he were breaking rocks); and, finally, in the fashion of Guy Lombardo, a long medley of Ellington numbers, all of them celebrated and lovely songs that were barely stated before being swept beneath the carpet to make way for the next number. The band, undismayed as always, played impeccably.

The major exceptions during the two weekends were forceful. On the opening night, Al Minns and Leon James, the dancers, strutted, slid, stomped, and spun their way through eighteen jazz numbers, accompanied by recordings that included a Fletcher Henderson side, dating back to the thirties, with a piercing, majestic Roy Eldridge solo that, unfortunately, was the best thing of its kind during the whole Festival. They were followed by the Modern Jazz Quartet, which during half of its ten numbers battled a thunderstorm that pushed the rain right through the canvas. The results were tonic, for the group performed with a brashness and lift that brought each of its pieces

—particularly the "D & E. Blues," "I'll Remember April," "The Golden Striker," and the new "Festival Sketch"—into perfect balance, so that Connie Kay, Milt Jackson, and John Lewis formed a liquid moving counterpoint that in time seemed to effortlessly still the din. On the second night of the final weekend, the pianist Cecil Taylor, accompanied by Sylvester Gandy on bass and Dennis Charles on drums, played four of his own compositions. Taylor's music is, in the main, unclassifiable. It is an improvised atonal music that has jazz rhythms more often implied than stated, and forms that appear to be strictly his own. An expert, classically trained pianist, he plays with a hammering intensity that never lets the listener rest for a moment. The result is a passionate, often grinding mixture of sounds, occasionally reminiscent of a bulging sample case of modern classical music, which, chockablock, range from graceful, lyric Debussy arpeggios to angry staccato chords that leap back and forth two or three octaves at a time. Yet his work invariably *suggests* jazz through its rhythms and attack, and appears, excitingly and furiously, to be trying to force its way to a level that has only been hinted at in the work of such modernists as Charlie Mingus and George Russell. Throughout Taylor's performance, the audience fidgeted, whispered, and wandered nervously in and out of the tent, as if the ground beneath had suddenly begun to wobble.

August 16

ONE STEP FORWARD, TWO STEPS BACK

THE NERVIEST, most tenacious movement to emerge from all the bewildering backing and filling in the jazz of the past decade—which includes the birth of hard bop; the rise and fall of the cool school; the resurgence of such swing musicians as Coleman Hawkins, Ben Webster, Roy Eldridge, Vic Dickenson, Edmond Hall, and Jo Jones; the effort to revive New Orleans jazz; and the fitful activity of the few remaining big jazz bands—has been the intense laboratory work of the small but steadily increasing group of experimental composers and arrangers, that includes Charlie Mingus, Jimmy Giuffre, John Lewis, Gerry Mulligan, Teddy Charles, Gil Evans, and George Russell. Starting with the basic belief that jazz can be composed—an assumption long ago proved by Jelly Roll Morton and Duke Ellington—these men have attempted, in compositions that often have no improvisation at all, to broaden its harmonic, rhythmic, and structural boundaries, as well as to widen its content. At the same time many of them have resurrected, in new and vigorous ways, collective improvisation, a kind of jazz that began going under in the late twenties, when the first great soloists appeared. (One of the fundamental elements of jazz is the tug of war—to say nothing of the resulting differences of mood and timbre—that occurs between the interdependence of collective playing and the lone-bird freedom of the soloist.) During most of the thirties and early forties, jazz grew more and more lopsided as it became, often against the largely static backdrop of the big band, an exhibition ground for such men as Louis Armstrong, Hawkins, Sidney Catlett, Benny Goodman, Sidney Bechet, Art Tatum, and Charlie Parker. It was almost immediately obvious, in many of their solos, which turned out to be little more than repetitions or variations of past flights, that there is nothing rarer than fresh jazz improvisation. Then, late in the forties—as if in reaction to this, as well as to bebop, with its daring, demanding melodic lines and complex, humpy rhythms—many young jazz musicians plunged into formal musical training. The fireworks have been going off ever since. Within the framework of the Modern Jazz Quartet, John Lewis has gone in for interplay and such devices as the rondo and the fugue; Giuffre has experimented with an implied rather than a sounded beat, with (like Mulligan) a careful, almost bemused counterpoint, and with lyrical blues-folk themes largely foreign to jazz; Mingus' preoccupation with the content of his music, which is often satiric and bitter, has resulted in his abandoning (like Charles) conventional chorus structures for his own patterns, the invention of weird chord sequences upon which to improvise, and the use, for certain effects, of the human voice, foghorns, taxi horns, and so on; Evans has developed new instrumentations and tonal colors; and Russell has employed atonality, broken rhythms, and solos as organic outgrowths—rather than battling opposites—of the ensemble. Some of this has been exciting, but much of it has been depressing. For this music has inevitably resulted in preciousness, musical tricks, the stifling of spontaneity, pure dullness, an over-attention to form, and a general solemnity and self-consciousness. It has often seemed, in fact, as if jazz—so graceful, surprising, and elusive at its best—might eventually evaporate, like a restless hired man.

That is pretty much what happens on a new Columbia record, "Modern Jazz Concert," a pretentious, exasperating, but occasionally brilliant and always ambitious collection of six compositions commissioned by Brandeis University, and played last year at its Festival of the Arts. Of the six composers, three are classical (Gunther Schuller, Milton Babbitt, Harold Shapero) and three jazz (Mingus, Russell, Giuffre). All the pieces are played by a cumbersome fourteen-piece group that includes two saxophones (John La Porta and Hal McKusick), two trumpets (Art Farmer and Louis Mucci), a trombone (Jimmy Knepper), a flute, a bassoon, a French horn, a harp, a vibraphone (Teddy Charles), a piano (Bill Evans), a guitar, a bass, and drums. Although the album notes, by Schuller, include an admirable map of what goes on, they also state, as in a vision, "Perhaps this is jazz or perhaps it is not. Perhaps it is a new kind of music not yet named." Perhaps, on the other hand (with a little boiling and scraping), it is this: one fairly successful jazz composition (Russell's "All About Rosie"); an obtuse atonal contrapuntal classical piece (Babbitt's "All Set"); a concoction in which, through sheer cleverness and compositional strength, jazz and classical music are forced together (Schuller's "Transformation"); a watery work that never, except in one brief instance, makes up its mind where it belongs (Shapero's "On Green Mountain"); and a couple of pieces (Giuffre's "Suspensions" and Mingus' "Revelations, First Movement") that are variations on jazz material that their composers have handled better elsewhere.

"All About Rosie" is, though at times a peculiarly cold work (much of Russell's composing has the same chilly, detached air), a frequently exhilarating effort. The first of its three movements is an up-tempo, semi-contrapuntal development, by the ensemble, of an Alabama folk song. The second is a sort of slow blues, with an attractive introduction that has several of the horns skating slowly through an atonal section, which, when finally resolved, turns into a slowly building pattern of riffs delivered in a dragging round, with a sharp afterbeat by the drummer, that eventually reaches a relentless, thumping conclusion. (The orchestration, however, is as colorless as it is throughout the record.) In the final movement, the folk theme is taken up again at a faster tempo by the ensemble until—bang!—in comes Evans for an improvised solo, which is a fascinating stomping effort, with fresh blues figures and a couple of passages where he suddenly shifts into a lolling half time, as if he were trying to drag the rhythm to a halt.

The best part of Shapero's rather dandyish "On Green Mountain," which is based on a chaconne by Monteverdi, is also its brief improvised section. Art Farmer, in the course of four choruses on the eight-bar theme, states the melody, embellishes it, then turns to a half-tempo improvisation and, in his last go-round, lets loose with a full set of up-tempo improvisations. (This is the only time in the entire record when anything imaginative is done with improvisation, which nearly all modern jazz composers, in their avidity for form, have ignored. Such possible departures as these have been largely bypassed a solo like the Farmer one, but in an extended sequence of direct melodic statement, embellishment, improvisation, embellishment, and a return to the original melody, done in a gradual form of crescendo and diminuendo; the use, within compositions such as "All About Rosie," of the harmonic and rhythmic methods of such soloists as Thelonious Monk, Cecil Taylor, and Sonny Rollins; a development of the extraordinary rondo-and-variations structure of some of Morton's piano solos; two solo instruments improvising at once, on the same or different themes.)

Schuller's "Transformation" begins as an unadorned classical piece in which a short, simple melody is repeated individually, as a slightly varied ground, by the horns, while the piano and drums inject clumps of jazz rhythms. By the time the theme is fully stated by the ensemble, the rhythm section has broken into a four-four gallop, which, in turn, dissolves into another first-rate Evans solo. This is overpowered by a lunging, shimmying riff that comes gradually out of the background. Then the rhythm slowly breaks into pieces, and there is a shift back to a classical design. It is a perfect, and totally unconvincing, tour de force.

September 13

M. BECHET

Although Sidney Bechet, the serene, high-domed, slightly Oriental-looking clarinettist and soprano saxophonist from New Orleans, has been in France for a decade (where he has successfully launched, at the age of nearly seventy, a new career as a music-hall performer), the gap he has left on this side of the ocean has never quite closed. One reason is its size. For, by the early forties, Bechet had been elevated to the aerie occupied by men like Louis Armstrong, Bunny Berigan, Art Tatum, and Coleman Hawkins. This was brought about by an obfuscating swarm of praise (from the moldy figs) and dismissal (from the modernists), which appeared to enlarge him, the way a fog seems to swell a house or a ship. As a result, when Bechet left for Europe there was general agreement on at least one thing: no matter what else, he was big. Part of this distortion has been Bechet's own unintentional doing. More than any other major soloist in jazz, he has made a basically unsentimental music come extremely close to the romantic—a magnetic, invariably troubling conversion, which usually draws either all slings or all hugs. Primarily, Bechet's style has a plump, passionate, skating quality. On the soprano saxophone, an instrument that, in the wrong hands, is apt to sound like faulty brakes, he has an impenetrable, almost teeming tone. An embellisher more than an improviser, he may, at fast and medium tempos, pour out straight melody like maple syrup, or stretch it into a series of commanding, sometimes shouting, legato phrases, or break it up into tight, chuffing staccato bits that occasionally turn into dirty, coruscating growls, as if they had been dipped in acid. (At very slow speeds, Bechet generally sticks close to the melody, which he is apt to deliver in an alternating series of moos and whoops.) What gives Bechet's lyricism its unique accents, while also appearing to shake it into one piece, is his vibrato, an astonishing device that, in its width and intensity, often resembles the phrase endings of an overheated diva. Bechet's clarinet playing, on the other hand, is a kind of antidote. Because of the compressing tonal limitations of the instrument, he is reduced to warm, eloquent pools of sound that, particularly in the blues, result in a melancholy capable of approaching pure misery. (Bechet is one of the few great blues soloists; essentially a primitive performer, like Armstrong, he seems almost magisterially at home within its one-two-three chord structure.) But this restraint never lasts long; his tone on the instrument eventually turns querulous and sharp, as if, unbearably impatient, he were trying to escape from a cramped, crowded room.

Bechet's outsize style long ago made him as unclassifiable as Armstrong, Tatum, and Hawkins. Yet he has frequently been regarded as a New Orleans type of performer, despite his brilliant recordings made in the thirties and forties, which, more often than not, include swing musicians such as Sidney Catlett, Sandy Williams, Sidney de Paris, Charlie Shavers, and J. C. Higginbotham, playing in the loose, collective style then fashionable for small-band recordings. Such baggy, slightly freakish surroundings suit Bechet perfectly. For when he is playing the saxophone, either in ensemble or in solos, he generally flattens everyone else on hand, through sheer volume and aggression. (The most conspicuous exception is a recording he made for Victor of "I Found a New Baby," in 1932, in which the terse, almost timid trumpeter Tommy Ladnier, apparently exercised beyond endurance by Bechet, loudly and alarmingly roars again and again into the upper register. The contest is exhilarating.)

Bechet is first-rate in a recording made not long ago in Paris and called "Sidney Bechet Has Young Ideas" (World Pacific Records). On hand, at Bechet's wish, is a mixed bag of modern musicians—the French pianist Martial Solal, Pierre Michelot or Lloyd Thompson on bass, and Kenny Clarke or Al Levitt on drums. The balance between Bechet's old lyrical flourishes and the chopped, right, boppish accents of his accompaniments is just about ideal; both parties seem to be continually and jovially correcting each other. There are fourteen tunes, all of them compactly handled standards done largely in medium tempos. (Bechet's choosing standards, rather than Dixieland tunes, is true to form; many of his earlier records are refashionings of numbers like "Rose Room," "Lady Be Good," and "Sweet Lorraine." It is a pity, though, that there are no blues on the record.) Bechet plays only the saxophone, and in a thoughtful, rather subdued way floats lazily through most of his material, varying puffs of melody with gently pressing variations. The most successful moments occur in "The Man I Love," which Bechet drives down as if it were a blues, and "These Foolish

Things Remind Me of You," which, taken at a slightly faster tempo than it usually is, has a Bechet solo that booms along and then, just as one is prepared for an explosion, drains away in a series of rude, growling two-bar exchanges with Solal, who, in turn, supplies an endlessly surprising combination of suspended tremolos, crooked, fleeing runs, and stark bass chords. Solal, indeed, is a constant delight. The rest of the rhythm section is lively, if jagged, with the exception of Clarke, whose accompaniments always resemble a steady, admiring stream of whispers. In fact it was Clarke who, with Bechet in 1940, first recorded in the style that, a year or two later, produced the revolutionary quicksands of bebop drumming. Bechet paid no mind.

For no apparent reason, four celebrations of the blues singing of Bessie Smith have appeared simultaneously—"La Vern Baker Sings Bessie Smith" (Atlantic), "Juanita Hall Sings the Blues" (Counterpoint), "The Legend of Bessie Smith: Ronnie Gilbert" (Victor) and "Dinah Sings Bessie Smith" (EmArcy). In the main, they only reaffirm her matchlessness. Miss Baker is the best of the lot. Accompanied by three groups that provide inspired work (despite some rather ponderous arrangements) by such men as Vic Dickenson, Buck Clayton, Urbie Green, and Jimmy Cleveland, she shouts, groans, and strains her way through twelve numbers, one of which, "Baby Doll," is given a wonderful rocking quality. Miss Hall, who is superbly backed by, among others, Coleman Hawkins and Doc Cheatham, played Bloody Mary in *South Pacific*, and she is a good musical-comedy shouter, while Ronnie Gilbert, a folk singer, handles her material with a round, mushroomy voice reminiscent of Kate Smith. Dinah Washington, a stylized, hard-voiced singer, whose work is built largely on technical tricks, is smothered by inept, ricky-ticky accompaniment—an apparent attempt either to copy or make fun of the original, sometimes classic support given Bessie Smith—that in places has all the push of Shep Fields and His Rippling Rhythm.

September 27

MORPHEUS AT BAY

THE STRANGEST and most ambitious part of "'Round About Midnight," a yawing, floppy concert given very early last Sunday morning at Loew's Sheridan Theatre, in Greenwich Village, was the premiere of a jazz opera, *Blues in the Subway,* with libretto and music by a thirty-one-year-old composer named Alonzo Levister. It was a solemn experience. Against a backdrop of the theater's middle-aged red-and-yellow curtains, which looked as if at some time they had accidentally been left out in the sun, and a life-size painting of the interior of a subway car (done in morose blues and blacks), the work was performed by three singers (Eva La O, soprano, Rolf Kristian, baritone, and Robert Battle, tenor) and four instrumentalists (the composer on piano, Shafi Hadi on tenor saxophone, Aly Mohammed Jackson on bass, and Danny Richmond on drums). Perched on tall wooden stools, the singers, who represented a boy, a girl, and a drunk, struggled with a misplaced microphone and a public-address system that suddenly developed a heavy, obliterating burr as they proclaimed—in a mixture of current Broadway music, Menotti, and who knows what else—such bits and pieces as "Wha station is this?," "I sick and tired," and "The Republicans are adamant, the Democrats are vehement, the Liberals are (inaudible), and the independents are perplexed." The drunk, who snoozed during most of the trip, kept waking up with a start, while the boy and girl did some largely muffled singing that involved an argument and a good deal of waving about of a newspaper. Except for brief solo excursions from the bass, drums, and horn, the accompaniment consisted of a rumbling, seemingly semi-improvised background that sounded as if it could have been played backward with identical results. After twenty minutes or so, the drunk, announcing that he had arrived at his stop, pulled a small, unidentifiable animal out of a bag and began to caress it while crooning a lullaby. The lights went down in the nick of time.

This curiosity (which did have the solid virtue of pointing out a refreshing musical possibility: the use of jazz and improvisation for the popular musical stage) was surrounded by three other groups. Backed by a trio, Anita O'Day opened the concert with ten songs, nine of which she sang expertly in her thin, parchmentlike voice. (The tenth was delivered in an apparently private key.) Although Miss O'Day invented most of the off notes and out-of-shape whoops and cries that Sarah Vaughan has made fashionable, she is not primarily a jazz singer. A small, lithe blonde, she has developed a rather hypnotic set of stage mannerisms that are reminiscent of the gracefully jerky, stylized movements of Balinese dancing. Indeed, it is as if she were trying to translate each of her songs into abstract physical patterns.

Next, the Tony Scott Quintet (the leader on baritone saxophone, Jimmy Knepper, Kenny Burrell, Jackson on bass, and Walt Bolden on drums) performed four numbers that were notable for Scott's nervous work (he is primarily a clarinettist), which consisted of pining leaps into the instrument's highest register, blatting bass honks, and crablike, middle-register runs—all done, nonetheless, with convincing heat—and for a fast version of "The Way You Look Tonight," a solo for Knepper, who, by combining oversized smears (some of them startlingly close to those often used by the Lombardo trombone section) with rapid, off-rhythm figures, frequently gave the peculiar impression of emitting a kind of furious, tumbling, subconscious melodic stream that, were it ever slowed down and sorted out, would provide enough material for two or three complete solos. Ben Webster joined Scott for three additional selections, and at least once—during his first chorus on a slow blues—produced a classic statement.

The opera was followed by Art Blakey's Jazz Messengers, which included Lee Morgan on trumpet and Benny Golson on tenor saxophone, along with a piano and bass. A memorable moment occurred during the medium "Blues March," when Morgan, matching Webster, played several choruses in a deft, lightning series of legato and staccato phrases so intertwined that they seemed, impossibly, to be happening simultaneously. Blakey, ordinarily a volcanic drummer, was remarkably subdued until the final number, "Night in Tunisia." Then, shifting to the tom-toms for some bellicose breaks, he abruptly pierced the drugged sleepiness within the house, which by this time had almost reached the level of a huge collective snore.

October 4

THE GREAT THINGS

THE TONE OF THE CONCERT given early last Friday evening in Carnegie Hall (and duplicated later that night) was pretty well set by the short, vacant opening remarks of its m.c., Symphony Sid, a disc jockey with a voice like a dredge: "It's so nice to have you here to listen to a lot of the great things I'm sure you'll enjoy." Symphony Sid then introduced the big hand of Ted Heath, ending with a fortissimo rumble into the microphone that was neatly incorporated into Heath's first number, an equally loud blues that had, among other things, a solo by the drummer, who kept his hands close together directly in front of his stomach as if he were expertly dealing an enormous pack of cards. (The band's movements were tic-like all evening: the bass player hovered all over his instrument, like a bee; the various sections ceaselessly stood up and sat down; the soloists ran from their seats to the microphone and back.) From all reports, Heath's band, which has sixteen pieces, is extremely popular in its native England, a country whose reverence for jazz has always seemed slightly improper. A brisk dance band that is a cross between Glenn Miller's and Jimmy Dorsey's (except for its rhythm section, which, by playing as if it were mopping the floor, suggested a rhythm section that Harry James had in the early forties), it ran through ten or so numbers, which included some stampeding; some well-tested solos; swelling renditions of "Star Dust," "Over the Rainbow," "High Noon," and "I'm Beginning to See the Light"; and a five-part suite. It then fell back to accompany half a dozen selections by its singer, Dennis Lotis, whose thin, slightly flat voice rattled through the hall like loose change. The band's final piece, a kind of rain dance, displayed the drummer soloing in total darkness with luminous drumsticks while the rest of the band waved phosphorized maracas around.

Ahmad Jamal, a thirty-eight-year-old pianist who hunches toward the keyboard as if he were proselytizing it, followed the intermission. Jamal is a genuine musical curiosity, whose style is vaguely akin to an attenuated version of Count Basie's. He will play some ordinary chords, drop his hands in his lap for ten measures, reel off a simple, rhythmic single-note figure (often in the high registers), drop his hands for five or six more measures, slip in an arpeggio, drop his hands again, plump off some new chords, and so forth—all of which eventually gives the impression achieved by spasmodically stopping and unstopping the ears in a noisy room. Accompanied by bass and drums, which sustained a heavy, warlike thrumming that seemed to frown on his efforts, Jamal played five numbers in this fashion, and after a time everything was blotted out but the attempt to guess when he would next lift his hands to hit the piano. It was trying work.

Dakota Staton, the singer, swam on almost immediately in a huge pale-blue bouffant dress that displaced about a quarter of an acre, and, backed by an unidentified quartet (piano, bass, drums, and flute or saxophone), delivered a dozen selections in a manner that moved precisely and unwaveringly between Sarah Vaughan (slow tempos) and Dinah Washington (fast tempos). Her enunciation, however, resembled a taffy pull. Symphony Sid closed the concert, just two and a half hours after it had begun, with some booming words that were lost in the sounds of the audience scrambling for the exits, lest it be caught again.

October 11

THE BEST MEDICINE

When Big Bill Broonzy, the dean of the old-time blues singers, died last summer, at the age of sixty-five, the *Times* printed a short notice near the middle of its obituary page, the area generally reserved for passé novelists and New Jersey businessmen. A few years ago, the late Art Tatum was given a resounding top-of-the-page two-column photograph and a statesman-length notice. The *Times* was right; the obituaries were accurate reflections of where the two men stood at the end of their lives. Thirty years ago, their positions would have been reversed. For although blues singing has been slowly and steadily declining ever since, it was regarded in the twenties with much the same enthusiasm as rock 'n' roll, a corruption of the blues, now is. (Peculiarly, instrumental blues now appear to be nearly as fashionable as vocal blues once were; during the past year alone over a dozen LPs have been devoted to them, to say nothing of the one or two blues that turn up on every new jazz record.) Nonetheless, Broonzy, who made hundreds of often obscure records, was widely and almost feverishly recorded before his death. Three of the efforts—"Big Bill Broonzy Sings Country Blues" (Folkways), "Big Bill Broonzy: The Blues" (EmArcy), and "Big Bill's Blues: Big Bill Broonzy" (Columbia)—all first-rate demonstrations of his later style, were set down in the past seven years but have only lately been released. They are a remarkable celebration of the blues.

Perhaps the best thing to do with our sporadically threatened national anthem, whose manhandling melody resembles a plain with a butte in the middle, would be to replace it with a good blues. The blues are indisputably American, they can be sung with ease, and they just about cover the register of human emotions. Nevertheless, they are usually considered a simple-minded song form that deals with anguish, dejection, or sorrow. There is good reason for this confusion. Washington Irving is credited with having first used the term "the blues" in 1807, as a synonym for melancholy: "He conducted his harangue with a sigh, and I saw he was still under the influence of a whole legion of the blues." His usage was a shortening of "the blue devils" (Robert Burns: "In my bitter hours of blue-devilism"; Thomas Jefferson: "We have something of the blue devils at times"), a synonym for a baleful presence that goes back at least to Elizabethan times, when blue apparently became associated with being down in the dumps. By the third quarter of the nineteenth century, both the non-musical term and the still nameless music derived from Negro spirituals, work songs, field hollers, and the like were in full swing, and since frequent characteristics of this music are slow rhythms and a seemingly minor harmonic cast, someone inevitably pasted them together. It was a poor alliance. Although the blues can express total gloom, as in

Blues, blues, blues, why did you bring trouble to me?
Blues, blues, blues, why did you bring trouble to me?
Oh, death, please sting me, and take me out of my misery,

they can also, as in many of the vocal and instrumental blues that began coming out of Kansas City in the early thirties, communicate an equally expressive buoyancy and abandon. Unlike the typical Anglo-American folk song, which has become largely picturesque and ornamental, the blues are still a functional music that is used both as elementary autobiography or confession (like all vital folk music) and/or as an emotional safety valve—for both the performer and the listener. At the same time, the blues can represent a kind of unspecified ill, which assumes a nearly visible shape, like the old blue devils themselves. The late Leadbelly once prefaced a song by saying:

> When you lay down at night, turn from one side of the bed all night to the other and can't sleep, what's the matter? Blues got you. Or when you get up in the mornin', and sit on the side of the bed—may have a mother or father, sister or brother, boy friend or girl friend, or husband or wife around—you don't want no talk out of um. They ain't done you nothin', and you ain't done them nothin'—but what's the matter? Blues got you. Well, you get up and shove your feet down under the table and look down in your place—may have chicken and rice, take my advice, you walk away and shake your head, you say, "Lord have mercy. I can't sleep, what's the matter?" Why, the blues still got you.

This process of catharsis is achieved in many ways. In vocal blues, anger can be got rid of with anger ("I can't eat the marriage license 'cause I ain't no billy goat [repeat]/I can laugh in your face and cut your doggone throat"); cruelty with satire or ridicule; disaster with humor ("If your house catch on fire, Lord, and there ain't no water around [repeat]/Throw your trunk out the window and let the shack burn down"); bereavement with selflessness ("That was the last time I saw my daddy's face [repeat]/Mama loves you sweet papa, wish I could take your place"); fear by disguising it in fable. Instrumental blues are an abstraction of vocal blues. With the comparative limitations of words, meanings, and the human voice removed (but with its image exaggerated by the horn), a good blues instrumentalist, like Louis Armstrong or Vic Dickenson, can, with delicate inflections, a wide range, and an inexhaustible variety of timbres—the growl, the mute, the thin, high-pitched note—seemingly revel in the persistent ache at the center of the blues. Moreover, the more elaborate, repetitive structure of blues singing, with its substructure of instrumental accompaniment, occasionally tends to become blurred and top-heavy, while a classic blues solo, like Armstrong's at the close of "Knockin' a Jug," a Columbia recording made in 1929, retains as sharp a sound as a slammed door. The most astonishing thing about the blues, that all-purpose medicine, is their ingenuity and simplicity.

The blues, which predate instrumental jazz, seem to have been specifically designed for jazz improvisation. Stripped to the essentials, the blues, which are a highly malleable form, have no set melody. A fairly common type developed in the thirties is most often twelve bars long and consists basically of three chords. In the key of B flat, a common one for blues, these chords are B flat, E flat seventh, and F seventh. They are arranged in a rough rondo form: B flat (four measures), E flat seventh (two measures), B flat (two measures), F seventh (two measures), and B flat (two measures.) The form moves toward a subtle climax with the F chord, and then slopes satisfactorily away to where it began. This pattern may be varied by all kinds of sub-chords, breaks, and ornamental notes. It is repeated again and again during a performance, so that the climactic chord in each chorus is picked up and slightly heightened by the same chord in the next. (The blues, like bridge, allow no dabbling; you feel them hotly or not at all.) But the mysterious emotional pull of the blues also resides in the so-called "blue notes," slightly flattened ones that frequently occur in the second and fourth chords; they may, however, appear in any of the chords. At slow tempos, these notes, in combination with the continually revolving tonic-subdominant-dominant form, can pleasurably evoke just about anything—a black-and-white November twilight, the longing bound up in the steam whistle, wind coming up in the trees. This air of Balkan melancholy, however, is sublimated at fast tempos, so that the harmonic structure becomes only a short, brisk, but still highly flexible form upon which to improvise.

Good lyrics rarely read well, just as good poetry is rarely set successfully to music. Despite their frequently being celebrated as a unique and beautiful folk poetry, blues lyrics are not often an exception. They are occasionally in a rough iambic pentameter, which is set in queer couplets whose first line is repeated twice. Broonzy had a disarmingly logical explanation for this:

> There's a lot of people can understand English, but you gotta talk very slow. So, the blues singers, they sing the same thing over twice. The same thing. Over and over again. No matter 'cause you're dumb, but simply to give you a chance to catch it the next time when they come around.

Blues lyrics usually don't scan, have faulty, strained rhymes, are repetitive and ungrammatical, and abound in nonsequiturs. Yet they sometimes come close to the concision of rhythms, words, and imagery of genuine poetry. There is a kind of one-armed poetry in this graceful brevity:

If you see me comin', hoist your window high.
Oh, if you see me comin', hoist your window high.
And if you see me goin', hang your head and cry.

This terseness is intensified, in the following stanza, by the words "railroad iron" and "pacify" and by the insistent, almost stuttering middle-of-the-line breaks:

I'm gonna lay, lay my head—yes,
On some sou-, southern railroad iron,
I'm gonna let that two, two-nineteen, dear,
Pacify my mind.

Through a Biblical foreshortening of space and time, parts of Bessie Smith's "Backwater Blues" achieve a rough majesty:

When it thunders and lightnin's, and the wind
begin to blow,
When it thunders and lightnin's, and the wind
begin to blow,
There's thousands of people ain't got no place
to go.

Then I went and stood up on some high old lonesome
hill,
Then I went and stood up on some high old lonesome
hill,
Then I looked down on the house where I used to
live.

Totally different is Muddy Waters' "Honey Bee," with its possibly unconscious parody of a poem that used to be drummed into every fifth-grader in America:

> Sail on, sail on, my little honey bee, sail on,
> Sail on, sail on, my little honey bee, sail on.
> You gonna keep on sailin' till you lose your
> happy home.

Thus, the real lyricism of vocal blues is a careful balance of the quality of the words, the particular melody hit upon, and the mood and technique of the performer. As in any fine mechanism, the parts are inseparable.

The first of the two great blues periods began around the turn of the century and ended about 1930. It involved two quite different groups. The earlier was the "country" blues singers, who, like Broonzy, worked their way all over the country as laborers, and, like genuine troubadours, recorded their adventures in their blues. (Parallel with them are the pioneer blues pianists, like Montana Taylor, Romeo Nelson, Pinetop Smith, Jimmy Yancey, and Cripple Clarence Lofton, who, though they occasionally sang, were primarily instrumentalists whose work, ironically, became well known only because of their best pupils—Albert Ammons, Pete Johnson, and Meade Lux Lewis.) They were, in the main, rough-and-ready singers whose voices often resembled foghorns and whose enunciation was unintelligible. Operating on the fringe of show business, they frequently adopted pseudonyms—the Yas Yas Girl, Speckled Red, Sunny Land Slim, Memphis Minnie, and Washboard Sam. Paradoxically, their blues were far more complex in structure and meaning than those of the "city" blues singers, who form the second group. For some reason, the best of the early "city" blues singers were women, among them Chippie Hill, Ida Cox, Sara Martin, Ma Rainey, and the unrelated Smith girls (Bessie, Clara, Trixie, Mamie, and Laura). All in all, Bessie Smith has never been equaled. A big monument of a woman, with a hard, handsome face, she had a thick contralto voice that seemed to threaten almost everything she sang. At the same time, her lumbering deliberation had a serenity and majesty—the majesty, in part, of sheer mass—that can be approximated only in opera. By 1930 many of these singers were dead or in obscurity, and the second blues period began. In one of its two groups are such singers as Jimmy Rushing, Joe Turner, Hot Lips Page, Teddy Bunn, and Jack Teagarden. They are, for the most part, more adept technicians, but they also have less of the sorrowing, brimstone quality of their predecessors. The second group includes the great blues instrumentalists, who, curiously, are also the great jazz musicians, the spirit of the blues having become the cornerstone of jazz. In recent years, these men have been almost savagely ignored by the members of the "funky" or "hard-bop" school, who go at the blues with hook and claw. Although they unintentionally capture some of the dreadnaught quality of the older men, their doggedness disrupts much of the delicate balance of parts that gives the form its poignancy. (The cool musicians, on the other hand, seem to cautiously pat the blues, as if they might get bitten.)

Like the older blues instrumentalists, the older blues singers have not, by and large, been surpassed. In fact, with the exception of such recent arrivals as Little Walter, a demonic singer and harmonica player; Joe Williams, a loud imitation of a blues singer; and the highly erratic

Ray Charles, new blues singers have simply stopped appearing. (An indirectly related form, gospel singing, appears, however, to be booming.) Perhaps the principal reason is that blues singing—passed orally from generation to generation—once filled an emotional gap that, even in the remote backlands of the South, is now inexplicably taken up by jukeboxes, radio, and television. In comparison, the old blues sound as archaic and unwieldy as Chaucerian English.

During the forty years that Broonzy sang the blues, he composed three hundred songs and provided a model for countless singers, the best known of whom is Josh White. He made his living not from singing or composing but by working as everything from a farmhand to a janitor, a necessity commemorated in such pieces as "Plough-Hand Blues" and "Mopper's Blues." Although his uncut baritone lost some of its resilience and lightness before he died, the outlines of his spacious technique are clearly visible in the three dozen selections on the Folkways, Columbia, and EmArcy records. "Trouble in Mind," an eight-bar blues on the Folkways record, is a superb example. Most blues singers rely on an unvarying method of attack, the boisterous shout. Broonzy, however, has a continual awareness of dynamics, dramatics, and shifting rhythm that is faultless. Here is the first stanza of "Trouble in Mind":

> I'm troubled in mind, baby, I'm so blue,
> Yes, but I won't, won't be blue always,
> You know the sun, sun gonna shine
> In my back door someday.

Singing at a very slow tempo, Broonzy delivers the first line almost as an aside, neatly squeezing all the syllables into about a measure, with a vague emphasis on the word "mind." Then, abruptly, he shouts the "yes" at the start of the next line, unbearably sustaining it on one note for two measures, until one gets the feeling of being pushed bodily backward. He cuts off the shout as suddenly as it begins (Broonzy used almost no vibrato) and eases through the rest of the line in a rapid, plaintive, gradually melting way. His voice continues to sink until the last line, which he half shouts in such a way that the emphasis curves up to the words "back door," and then subsides. The total effect of the stanza is of slow, deliberate, slightly irregular hammer strokes. Broonzy's own "I Wonder When I'll Get to Be Called a Man," a social-protest blues, on the same record, which goes, in part,

> When I got back from overseas,
> That night we had a ball,
> Next day I met the old boss,
> He said, "Boy, you get some over-hauls!"

is sung at a rolling medium tempo, but in a delicate, off-hand way that inescapably points up the meaning of the lyrics. In "Texas Tornado" (on the Columbia record), he reverts to the classic blues-singing style—a sustained shout, with a slight dropping of the voice at the end of each of the first two lines, followed by the quieter, resolving third line. His treatment fits the words nicely:

> My baby is a Texas tornado, and she howls just
> like the wind.
> My baby is a Texas tornado, and she howls just
> like the wind.
> She'll blow the house down, Lord, if I ask her
> where she been.

Broonzy, however, is incomparable in "Southbound Train," which appears on both the EmArcy and Folkways records. It is sung slowly and gently all the way through, each word sliding into the next, as if being hummed. (Broonzy backs himself on guitar on all three records, except for five numbers in the EmArcy album, in which he is accompanied by a small, thumping blues band.) The melancholy in his voice never varies, but because of the inexorable blues pattern it seems to deepen steadily. By the time he has reached the last two stanzas—which, though, unashamedly emotional, are not, as is true of all blues, the least sentimental—one is reduced to a state of solid compassion:

Standin' at the station, tears was in my eye.
Standin' at the station, tears was in my eye.
Now that I've lost my best friend, how can I be
satisfied?

I hear a whistle, wonderin' where is that train.
I hear a whistle, wonderin' where is that train.
Now that I've lost my baby, I've got all red
brain.

Broonzy fills in the pauses between lines with bright, quiet staccato strummings that provide a stunning contrast to the fiber of his voice. Indeed, the balance between voice and guitar, form and content, and emotion and restraint is perfect. It's a pity the *Times* was right.

October 25

AN EVENING IN BROOKLYN

"JAZZ '59," a concert held last Friday at the Brooklyn Academy of Music, a huge battleship-gray hall whose ceiling disappears in a haze of boxes, balconies, nymphs, harps, and eagles, turned out to be one of the palest confections ever put together in these parts. The evening was divided up by various mysterious and apparently arbitrary parlor-music combinations of one basic group—Zoot Sims, Sam Most (alto saxophone and flute), Gil Melle (baritone saxophone), Marian McPartland, Mose Allison, Teddy Charles (vibraphone, piano, and bongo drums), Joe Cinderella (guitar), and two alternating bassists and two alternating drummers—which ceaselessly came together and drifted apart in such a way that the opening group, made up of practically the entire personnel, was succeeded by baritone saxophone and rhythm (with a different drummer), which was followed by vibraphone and rhythm, which was followed by a singer, Barbara Lea, with the same rhythm, who was followed by flute (with the same rhythm minus the guitar and plus Charles on the piano), and so forth. The effect, within the immensities of the place, was of an undermanned, besieged outpost going about tasks usually apportioned among three times as many people. After the initial selection, a jumpy, indifferent rendition of "Oh, Lady Be Good," which was announced as a Thelonious Monk arrangement but could have been fashioned not long ago in Kansas City, Melle, a towering, stooped man, who made his instrument look as if it would fit easily into his pocket, played three of his own compositions, doing battle most of the way with Cinderella, whose amplifier had the volumes of a ten-man Hawaiian ensemble. (Melle was also forced to tow his drummer, a thin, mustached man who strikingly resembled a peevish Nasser and kept lowering the beat.) A vigorous, subtle performer, given to soft runs and plaintive legato figures, Melle, when audible, was at his best in "Full House," a medium-tempo blueslike number. Teddy Charles followed with several selections that sounded like the outlines for finished performances, and gave way to Miss Lea, who enunciated four numbers in a clear, small voice that effortlessly recalled Lee Wiley. Sam Most, on the flute, appeared, and in "It Might as Well Be Spring" attempted to simultaneously hum what he was playing. The result was like a radio tuned in to two stations at once.

The concert began to develop a little color in its cheeks midway in its second half when Sims, who uses a rough, emotional variation of Lester Young's closeted tone, played three numbers, including a slow, walloping rendition of "Willow Weep for Me." Marian McPartland, accompanied by bass and drums, mixed handfuls of splashing chords with flat, stainless, single-note passages, frequently making room for solo drum passages full of rapid, precise riveting sounds. The entire cast, minus a bassist and drummer, returned for the closing selection, "Night in Tunisia," which was performed in diminuendo. Then Miss McPartland, who had acted as a part-time m.c., thanked the audience, and, standing front and center, was tunked on the head by the falling curtain, which crept almost reluctantly back into the air, as if it, too, had tired blood.

November 8

MORELLO THE MIGHTY

LIKE A WITHERING balloon, the Dave Brubeck Quartet has been slowly but surely changing shape in the two years since Joe Morello took over as its drummer. Before that, the group, which also includes Paul Desmond and Gene Wright (bass), had been almost totally overshadowed by its leader, a tall, shambling, hawk-nosed man who often started enormous solos with simple single-note figures and ended in masses of wandering Floating Island chords. Desmond, a thin, equally tall man who, when he is not playing, folds his hands over his saxophone as if it were a paunch, generally rushed in at either end of a number to pit his small, buttery tone against Brubeck for some absorbing counterpoint and fugue. But all this has changed. A powerful, precise drummer, with a left hand as furious as an electric typewriter, Morello, whether because of his bobsledding movements or because of their abrasive action on Brubeck and Desmond, has been gradually obliterating the rest of the group. Indeed, what one chiefly hears in almost every selection are brilliant snare-drum work (Morello's rimshots pop like a whip), glistening cymbal patterns, and massive, irregular arrays of bass-drum beats, like elephants dancing, while, somewhere in the background, Brubeck and Desmond provide wistful, barely supporting accompaniment.

Much of this was in evidence in the Quartet's performance during the first of two concerts, called "Jazz for Moderns," last Friday evening at Carnegie Hall. It seemed like old times during the early part of the group's first number, the "St. Louis Blues." Desmond took a long, tiptoeing solo, Brubeck began his portion by noodling and closed with some bearlike arguments, and then, as if waking from a dream, suddenly petered out into pianissimo figures as Morello swelled up behind him and burst into a brief, drenching solo that brought everything back to the present. Six numbers later, after a couple of ballads, a variation on Bach, and an Afghanistan-flavored affair (in which Morello again rose up imperiously), Morello launched a five-minute outburst, driving Brubeck and Desmond out of their positions and behind the piano, where they remained, in waiting, till its end.

The Brubeck group was preceded by the Sonny Rollins Trio (the leader, Henry Grimes on bass and Kenny Dennis on drums), which opened the evening in an unusual way by bringing it to an immediate climax. Playing just two standards and a blues, Rollins, whose coughing, braying tone has shifted into a full, domineering sound, was hypnotic. He is an improviser who, at the outset of just about every tune, invents a slight variation on its melody and uses that variation (rather than the chords of the melody) as a theme, which he turns over, pokes, pulls, slaps, throws into the air, and then restates, before again testing its resilience. He has also developed a sly, comic approach by frequently intoning his variations in a slightly bleary, sidling way, falling away from each note as if it were slippery. His performance was tantalizingly short.

Sliding steadily downward, the concert neared bottom,

after Brubeck and the intermission, with Maynard Ferguson's twelve-piece band, which, dressed in bright-red jackets and stationed behind squat, dark-gray music stands that resembled toadstools, performed five selections with a venomous power that was continually fanned by Ferguson's loud, high winds. This gave way to the Four Freshmen, a quartet that sounded like a one-man band and accompanied itself on trumpet, trombone, mellophone, guitar, bass, and drums while exchanging jokes and singing such things as "Sweet Lorraine" in a mousy falsetto, and an unbelievably lachrymose rendition of Willard Robinson's "Old Folks," which deals with an old man ("children's voices at play will be stilled for a day, the day that they take Old Folks away"). Then the Ferguson band, which had sat by in a sagging, stony silence during the Freshmen's eleven numbers, erupted again, as if uncaged, into a brisk blues and a medley of Broadway tunes that were so uninhibited it took some time for its final chord to die away.

November 15

THE DEVIL AND THE DEEP BLUE SEA

WITH THE EXCEPTION OF the bright, needling, occasionally even truculent work of Charlie Mingus, Thelonious Monk, Gil Evans, and John Lewis, most modern jazz has begun to swing aimlessly back and forth between a sloppy monotony and an Edwardian fastidiousness, and when both are heard at one sitting they sometimes have the frustrating effect of simply canceling each other out, like double penalties. More often than not, the solos, engendered both by the practically limitless playing time of the LP and by an apparently compulsive garrulity, are far too long. At the same time, the soloists are frequently only Japanese-made imitations of their elders and betters. And muffling all, like a soundproof ceiling, are the still-lingering fashion of cool playing, which forbids everything but the offhand and the oblique, and an overabundance of technique, which makes a good many modernists sound as if they were doing algebra out loud. The result is that emotion, the seat of all music, must be ceaselessly grappled for by the listener.

Much of the Edwardian approach was in evidence one evening a week or so ago in the McMillin Theatre, at Columbia, where the Gerry Mulligan Quartet (Art Farmer, Bill Crow, bass, and Dave Bailey, drums), augmented for part of the time by several ringers (Jerome Richardson, alto saxophone and flute, Jimmy Cleveland, and Jimmy Jones), performed eighteen numbers with an indefatigable, highly polished deliberation. Largely because of Farmer, who is moving unerringly away from the muscle-bound aspects of bebop toward a precise and penetrating lyricism, this is the best of the various quartets Mulligan has had in the past four years. (Bailey, however, is unremittingly dull, a habit that is enthusiastically shared by most of his colleagues on the instrument.) Nonetheless, almost half of its numbers—such things as "Moonlight in Vermont," "Line for Lyons," "My Funny Valentine," and "Bernie's Tune"— were only slightly readjusted versions of the original quartet's repertory, while much of the sudsy romanticism that used to rise, now and then, to genuine lyricism was replaced by the staleness of too much practice. (This is particularly noticeable in Mulligan's playing. An offshoot of Lester Young and Charlie Parker, he is an extremely adept musician who, though he invariably plays with great energy, ends by issuing retreads of phrases that have already clocked a good many miles. And now missing are the selectivity of notes and the sense of dynamics that once produced a rather touching eloquence.) Just after the intermission, Richardson, Cleveland, and Jones joined the others, music stands were hauled out, and the enlarged group swelled smoothly through five selections by Johnny Mandel taken from the sound track of the motion picture *I Want to Live*. It was West Coast jazz—pleasant, fragmentary melodies, stagy ensembles, filler solos—at its most vacuous. The quartet returned for three numbers, and in a brisk reworking of the "Bugle Call Rag," titled "Blueport," in which Mulligan and Farmer traded a complex series of six-bar breaks

(Farmer, in particular, playing with a brilliantly controlled steam), it seemed, at last, as if the group were about to disclose its closest secrets.

The first of two concerts held last Friday at Town Hall, and displaying the Jimmy Giuffre 3, Mulligan, the Thelonious Monk Quartet, and Miles Davis' sextet, was a classic demonstration of the canceling-out process. Giuffre's trio (the leader on tenor saxophone and clarinet, Jim Hall, and Bob Brookmeyer) opened the evening with a blues that, in contrast to his usual creations, which sometimes resemble inner monologues recited simultaneously by three people, consisted of simple opening and closing ensembles and long, fervent solos. After delivering some soft, crackling figures behind Giuffre, Brookmeyer slid into a couple of choruses of half-valved sounds and husky glissandos that recalled the old Dickie Wells. It was a stirring solo. Giuffre took off on the clarinet in the next number, "Stella by Starlight," and, abandoning his customary lower register, where he tends to shuffle moodily around like a truffle hog, stepped all over his keys. But then the freeze set in. Giuffre's final numbers reverted to his studied manner, and this was carried forward by Mulligan's eight selections, more than half of them again given over to the sound-track music (played, once more, by a larger group), which, perhaps because of the acoustics of the hall, sounded far fleshier than it had a week earlier. Then, for three brief numbers, Monk's group, with Charlie Rouse on tenor saxophone, Ahmed-Abdul Malik on bass, and Roy Haynes on drums, burst through. Monk's work, especially on "In Walked Bud," an up-tempo composition, was a memorable concatenation of bodily movements (slapping, dancing feet; poking, partially extended fingers that suggested a doctor prodding a nerveless patient; violent swaying motions that nearly pitched him into the instrument) and dissonant, delayed-action figures, thudded out, again and again, in the high registers, with slight rhythmic and harmonic variations, through almost an entire chorus, as if, by God, he would get it right yet, which, of course, he did. Davis' group, which includes John Coltrane and Julian Adderley followed, and, in the space of just three selections, unraveled steadily (Coltrane's grapeshot runs, Davis' repeated attempts to squeeze into the upper register, Adderley's flooding ruminations) until, in a fast number called "Billy Boy," played by Davis' pianist and bassist and the drummer Philly Joe Jones, everything fell apart, and the concert, canceled out, ended by vanishing into thin air.

December 6

THE SECRETS OF THE PAST

IT'S NOT OFTEN that a tour de force, by coming off badly, accomplishes more than it set out to do. But that's what happened one night last week at the Apollo Theatre, on 125th Street, when Herb Pomeroy's band, a sixteen-piece aggregation from Boston, attempted, in a concert called "The Living History of Jazz," to duplicate some of the multitude of jazz styles that have come and gone in the past sixty years. (The program was accompanied by a commentary written and spoken by John McLellan, a Boston disc jockey, that was largely "objective" opinion, pitted here and there with such phrases as "the tension-relaxation dichotomy.") Aside from the sheer bravery of it all, the imitations of such men as Louis Armstrong, Bix Beiderbecke, Baby Dodds, Roy Eldridge, Chu Berry, and Count Basie were just good enough to recall their wizardry and more than inept enough to underline the fact that their supposed simplicities often were, or are, far more inaccessible than the celebrated intricacies of their successors. As a result, the affair, which the band had been practicing up on, largely in New England, during the past couple of years, pointed up two melancholy facts: (1) that most modern jazz musicians are extraordinarily provincial about their own music, and (2) that by being so about most of the classic jazz that has gone before them they probably halve their own potentialities. The evening was saved from total ruin by the presence of half a dozen guests, some the genuine article (Sonny Terry, the forty-seven-year-old blues singer and harmonica player; Willie the Lion Smith, one of the last of the great Harlem stride pianists; and Candido, a conga drummer who uses his elbows, his nose, his feet, and the floor, with thunderous effect), and some long-time copyists (Sol Yaged, a Goodman imitator who is almost better at Goodman than Goodman was; Zoot Sims; and Big Miller, a diffuse blues singer who can't decide between Joe Turner and Jimmy Rushing).

The program started like a cannon shot with a blues by Terry, who alternately sang and backed himself on the harmonica, on which he created ferocious squeals while wildly whacking the instrument with his free hand, as if he were polishing a brass plate. Willie the Lion genially transmuted an example of ragtime ("The Maple Leaf Rag") and of James P. Johnson ("The Carolina Shout") into pure Willie the Lion. Then the mistakes began. A spasm band (washboard, bones, harmonica, and washtub bass) rattled along with all the force of a quilting bee. It was replaced by an imitation of the Buddy Bolden band, done in so loud an off-key shout that it became unintentional parody. Lennie Johnson, a trumpeter, went after Armstrong in "Sleepy Time Down South" and salvaged some of Armstrong's best mid-thirties clichés, while Pomeroy, also a trumpeter, tackled Beiderbecke in "The Royal Garden Blues" and, in his first few notes, almost had him. Two generally workaday rundowns of Ellington and Lunceford were capped by Yaged's spooky Goodman and a thin, papery rendition of the Basie band. Disaster followed. Eldridge, Berry, Dodds, Jo Jones, Kenny Clarke, and Miles Davis, among others, were badly smudged. (Eldridge was represented by some high-register rasps, and Dodds, one of the smoothest and craftiest of all drummers, by two quick, uneven snare-drum rolls.) These gave way, not unexpectedly, to extremely skillful copies of Charlie Parker, Dizzy Gillespie's big band of a decade ago, the Miles Davis-Gerry Mulligan group of the same period, Woody Herman's Third Herd, and one of Mulligan's recent quartets. Finally, the band, at last representing its occasionally first-rate self, played a fast blues, "The Opener," but, either exhausted by its archaeology class or just plain dispirited because of the demands this classwork had imposed, the group sounded pretty much like any second-class big jazz band—blatant, unfinished, and top-heavy. It made one pine for the old glories that the performers had, earlier in the evening, failed to master but that, along with their contemporaries, they are popularly believed to have improved upon.

December 20

PART FOUR

1959

MINGUS AMONG THE UNICORNS

LAST FRIDAY NIGHT, in the Nonagon Art Gallery, on lower Second Avenue—a long, narrow, second-floor room whose fireplace, brooding beams, heavy chandeliers, and dark woodwork carved with unicorns, lions rampant, and medieval heads give it the air of a Hohenzollern hunting lodge—the third in a superior series of monthly modern-jazz concerts was devoted to the Charlie Mingus Quintet. In addition to being a reaffirmation of the passionate intelligence Mingus has for several years been pouring into his work, it was perhaps the only first-rate affair of its kind held in New York since the Modern Jazz Quartet's Town Hall appearance last year. Fortunately, Mingus usually bears down with equal weight on his talents as composer, arranger, and bassist. He excels at fresh, poignant blues melodies and leisurely, almost ornate ballad numbers spelled out in long, graceful melodic lines that move as if they were being played in slow motion. He is an arranger who experiments continually with rhythm by supercharging his pieces with different but always related tempos, stop-time choruses, and complex double-time or staccato background effects whose near frenzy seems to endow whatever else is going on with a tranquillity and stateliness rare in modern jazz. He has also developed various raucous, rasping contrapuntal ensemble methods that, by persistently rubbing its melody the wrong way, fill the cheeks of the palest tune with color. Finally, Mingus has no peer, past or present, on the bass. He invariably gives the impression of accomplishing what the instrument was never intended for, and yet, peculiarly, it is not his virtuosity that one is hypnotized by but the daring and inimitable melodic and rhythmic content that is the result of it.

All of Mingus' sizable achievements—and his impressive bulk, which is approaching that of the late Sydney Greenstreet—were in evidence at the concert. On hand with him were Booker Erwin, tenor saxophone; John Handy, alto saxophone; Richard Wyands, piano; and Danny Richmond, drums. The first of the eight numbers, which ranged from seven to seventeen minutes, was a rather perfunctory medium up-tempo version of "Take the 'A' Train." It was followed by Mingus' attempt to capture the essence of Jelly Roll Morton—a direct forebear of Mingus—in a number called "Jelly Roll Jellies." Instead of being a celebration, the number turned into a clumsy takeoff; the saxophones mooed out a dolorous melody reminiscent not of Morton but of Art Hickman, and gave way to similarly parodying solos, which in turn evaporated into the various instrumentalists' own styles. The foolhardiest effort came from Richmond, who, before slipping into his own manner of playing, played several solo choruses, presumably modeled on Zutty Singleton and Baby Dodds, that made them into the world's least accomplished drummers. "Alice's Wonderland," a slow ballad by Mingus, with a wandering, thick-textured melody, followed, and it was, in contrast, a delight from beginning to end. After stating the melody, the horns, swelled abruptly by Mingus' humming in falsetto at the top of his lungs, slid into a weird, wavering descending figure, which was cut off by a short arrhythmic interlude, with the piano fashioning porous, Impressionistic chords, the drummer pinging on finger cymbals, and Mingus playing rapid strumming phrases. There was a swaggering, exaggerated restatement of the melody by the horns, then some good solos, and, finally, a repetition by the ensemble of the patterns used at the outset. It was a near-perfect piece. Handy was particularly striking. A young musician from San Francisco, he played with flawless control, and though the work of Charlie Parker forms a broad dais for his style, he used, unlike most of his colleagues on the saxophone, a highly selective number of notes, a warm tone, and a couple of devices—a frequently prolonged trill astonishingly like that of the old New Orleans clarinettist George Baquet, and ivory-like sorties into the upper register reminiscent of Benny Carter's smooth ascents—that set him several paces away from his first model. "Billie's Bounce," done at a brisk tempo broken by stop-time rhythms and double-time effects in the background, disintegrated halfway through into a drum solo, which, not surprisingly, was long, lurid, and loud. (Modern drumming, which evolved from the nervous, expertly turned inventions of Kenny Clarke and Max Roach, has exasperatingly become a separate solo tradition, in which the drummer wades wildly and unconcernedly through almost every number as if there were no one present but himself.)

After the intermission, a ten-minute rendition of "I Can't Get Started" was built around Handy and Mingus, who produced an extraordinary solo three or four choruses long and full of quick, two-steps-at-a-time clambering around the scale, lightning strummings, sometimes carried out with both hands, and slow, booming notes that seemed to bulge out the walls. The concert closed, after another Mingus ballad, with "Wednesday Night Prayer Meeting," a rocking blues founded on the accents and rhythms of gospel music, which were pulled back and forth by a variety of rhythms. These also had the effect of elevating, at regular intervals, the head of a Medusa-haired spectator inexplicably drowsing in the second row, not eight feet from a roaring Richmond.

The concert was recorded on the spot, and although several selections were interrupted for brief retakes and admonishments by Mingus to his musicians (to his drummer: "Don't get so fancy. This is *my* solo, man"), these diversions only accentuated the general vibrancy of the evening.

January 24

THE LAST OF THE MOHICANS

THE TRADITION of great solo jazz pianists—soloists to the extent of being virtual one-man bands—which began with the early blues and boogie-woogie pianists and was developed as an almost separate art by such men as Jelly Roll Morton, Earl Hines, James P. Johnson, Fats Waller, Art Tatum, Teddy Wilson, and Jess Stacy, has become hopelessly diminished. For despite its vast numbers, the army of modern jazz pianists that has inexplicably appeared in recent years (on an enormous number of LPs, each by a different performer) has almost nothing in common with its predecessors. Indeed, these pianists resemble a house of mirrors. Each reflects or distorts Bud Powell, Thelonious Monk, or Lennie Tristano—the only original pianists (with one notable exception) of the past decade—or, worse than that, copies the others. Not surprisingly, they have a common stylistic denominator. In the right hand, it consists of long, hard melodic lines in single notes, sounded like ping-pong balls (as opposed to, say, the almost angelic transparency of Stacy's celebrated unscheduled solo in the "Sing, Sing, Sing" played at Goodman's 1938 Carnegie Hall concert), or of thick, box-toed chords that clump heatedly and meaninglessly around the keyboard in staccato ranks. In the left hand, one finds largely inaudible murmurs, or spasmodic offbeats that tend to underline the essentially nervous, disconnected air of the right hand. The total effect is colorless, unfinished, metallic, and monolithic. The one exception to all this is Erroll Garner, the remarkable thirty-seven-year-old bravura pianist from Pittsburgh, who, though he is comparable to no one, belongs, in manner and scope, with Hines, Tatum, and Waller. Two recent releases, one involving the epitome of modern pianists, Hampton Hawes ("All Night Session! with the Hampton Hawes Quartet," Contemporary), and the other Garner ("Paris Impressions: Erroll Garner," Columbia), serve, respectively, as perfect illustrations of this current disease and what, for a time at least, seemed its antidote.

Garner is already a genuine legend. During the past fifteen years, he has made more solo records than any other jazz pianist, alive or dead (between five hundred and a thousand for well over seventy labels, some of which, it is said, stay in existence by simply pirating his records back and forth), including a recent release, "Concert by the Sea" (Columbia), that is reported to be one of the four or five most popular jazz records ever put out. (Garner is phenomenal in a recording studio; in a few hours he sometimes sets down, without pause or retakes, a dozen or more numbers, some of them eight or ten minutes in length.) The reasons for his Sinatralike acclaim are puzzling. It began, of course, with the near-adoration that, until not long ago, many admirers of jazz had for him. (Bohemian's law, that true art originates only in the garret, still operates to an astonishing degree in jazz; when an occasional jazz musician breaks into the big time, he immediately becomes suspect and, often as not, is dropped from all rolls of honor.) More than that, Garner's appeal probably stems not from his style, which is unbendingly rococo and eccentric, but from the easily accessible flash, geniality, and warmth that continually propel it—qualities that once contributed a good deal to the success of such otherwise second-rate musicians as Gene Krupa, Harry James, and Charlie Barnet. A short, ebullient, parrot-nosed man who invariably accompanies himself with an infectious and appreciative series of grunts, hums, buzzes, and exclamations ("Uh-huh," "Yahhm," "Oho"), which seem to double the already high emotional level of his music, Garner is a totally untutored musician who cannot read a note of music. Basically, his plush, pumping orchestral style is divided into two quite different approaches—the rhapsodic and the stomping. When Garner rhapsodizes, he ebbs and floods all over the keyboard, producing, with frequent use of the pedal, vaporous pillows of sounds, full of vague chords and trailing, blurred strings of notes. It takes a steady beat to marshal his peculiar characteristics. These involve an extraordinary, almost melodramatic sense of dynamics that no other jazz musician has dared use, and a shifting, highly distinctive rhythmic attack, both of which result in the transmission of pure lumps of emotion through an instrument that in jazz can be flatly inimical to eloquence.

Garner's introductions, which sometimes last eight bars, are often complete, if irregular, compositions in themselves. In a typical medium-tempo number, he may start with heavy, seesawing chords in the left hand that, pitted against his right hand, which repeats or improvises in broken rhythms upon a simple, sharply plucked figure, produces the tantalizing effect of rapid backing and filling. When the listener has been bullied into a cliff-hanging frame of mind (on top of all this, Garner's introductions never indicate what they are introducing), he abruptly slices his volume by two-thirds and drops lightly and offhandedly into the first chorus. Staying close to the melody, his right hand may play barely struck chords that lag just behind the beat, while his left hand settles into metronomic dum-dum-dum chords, each dropped precisely on the beat. Before the end of the chorus, he will slip back into jockeying, arrhythmic figures, increase his volume, drop it again, and slide into the next chorus, where his left hand begins frequently interrupting its strumming with sharp, perfectly spotted offbeats and his right hand starts dancing off marvelous, hoppity single-note patterns that leap through several octaves, continually circling the beat but never quite landing on it, as if it were electrified. Carrying an increased volume intact into the following chorus, he will shift into a complex of wobbling tremolo chords (right hand) and blocklike thumpings (left hand), which, when he reaches the bridge of the tune, he abruptly abandons for warring contrapuntal single-note lines, played by both hands. The final chorus, though often a simmering-down version of the first, often dissolves into a wandering, uneasy coda, which is suddenly clapped shut with a heavy chord, as if by a gust of wind.

For all its wonders, Garner's style, which has changed very little during the past decade, has become so rigidly perfect within its own terms that it borders on monotony. The nimble, devious single-note passages begin, after a time, to sound much alike, the jumbled, chorded interludes can be spotted miles away, the this-way, that-way rhythmic approach never gains in subtlety or variety, the tremolo chords (similar to those once used so effectively by the old-time blues pianists) reappear too often. The enormous vitality in his work seems, because it can find no new outlets, to be ceaselessly turning back on itself or getting out through variations of variations of the same old figures. Like any Mandarin stylist, Garner must be sampled, not swallowed.

That, in fact, is the best approach to his new album, which contains eighteen numbers, two-thirds of them his own celebration of a recent tour of France. He is accompanied throughout by bass and drums. The tempos are restricted to slow and medium, and in only a handful ("Left Bank Swing," "La Petite Mambo," and "The French Touch"), which include, in addition to some spirited single-note passages, several of his inimitable bridges (complete with assorted grunts), does he get down to business. This also happens when, for four selections, he shifts for the first time to the harpsichord. The results are memorable, especially in a slow, blueslike number of his own, "Don't Look for Me," in which, by using rapidly changing combinations of watery tremolos, by stating the melody in the left hand while banging out wild, spindly figures in the right, and generally reveling in the sonorities of the instrument, he manages to sound like a carillon booming Napoleon's defeat at Moscow.

Hampton Hawes, a thirty-year-old from the West Coast, is a one-man anthology of the rest of modern jazz piano. The "All Night Session" records, which were made two years ago during one long, uninterrupted evening, have been widely praised, probably more for their jam-session nature than for their musical content. Hawes, who is accompanied by Jim Hall, Red Mitchell on bass, and Bruz Freeman on drums, plays sixteen numbers, including an equal sprinkling of blues, standards, bop-era tunes, and his own numbers. The average playing time is over seven minutes, and there are a couple of numbers that last for eleven minutes. It's a remarkable six-day bicycle race. The records are a catalogue of the styles of a dozen pianists, including Horace Silver, Oscar Peterson, and Bud Powell (very strong), Monk and George Shearing (strong), and Johnny Williams and John Lewis (not so strong). What results is a tough, vigorous, sweating pastiche, which is at its most energetic in a long, medium-tempo blues, "Hampton's Pulpit" (Horace Silver kibitzing), and at its most meaningless in a fast "Groovin' High" (Oscar Peterson kibitzing). Hall is intelligent but subdued, as is Freeman, while Mitchell, a powerful, singing bassist who plays in the manner of Charlie Mingus, is direct and forceful. If it were not for his onward-and-upward manner, one might suspect Hawes of attempting a parody of all modern jazz piano. He'd have succeeded brilliantly.

January 31

P. W. RUSSELL, POET

THE TERM "moldy fig," which is one of the aptest derogatory colloquialisms in the language, was first used in jazz to describe those who believe that the music has been in steady decline since around 1930. But this moldy fig has lately been overshadowed by the new moldy fig, who, with white-lipped conviction, has moved the old limit up to 1945. (For the record, the new fig, who is, if possible, even more ferocious than his forebears about what has come since, flourishes best in England and France, where jazz has been hotly cherished almost from the day of its birth, and where, in the jazz press, he wages war with a rattling, medieval hauteur.) Although the myopia of these views, which damage no one but their possessors, is more than obvious, the most recent of them nonetheless stems from a sad truth—that the open-handed lyricism displayed by the great swing musicians who came to the fore between 1935 and 1945 is almost nonexistent in modern jazz. The new moldy fig rarely bothers explaining just what this undeniable lyricism was, or is, beyond repeatedly pointing out that men like Ben Webster, Pee Wee Russell, and Jess Stacy have an extraordinary poetry in their music. This magnetism, however, is caused by more than Webster's vibrato, Stacy's tremolos, and Russell's intensity, and by more, too, than their collective ability to "swing," a verb that has become so abstract that André Hodeir, a young French critic and composer, was forced in his recent book on jazz to the verge of higher mathematics in an attempt to define it. Perhaps, along with these essentials, to say nothing of mood, environment, sobriety, and good digestion, this lyricism is the result of two rather old-fashioned qualities—grace and artlessness. These appear when a musician like Russell miraculously and unselfconsciously translates such blueslike emotions as melancholy, yearning, and restlessness into a certain bent phrase or huskiness of tone with such surpassing timing and clarity that the listener suddenly becomes a transfixed extension of the musician—a transformation that Russell, a fifty-three-year-old from Missouri, has been mysteriously accomplishing, with increasing refinement and serenity, for many of the thirty-odd years of his career.

Unfortunately, Russell has almost always been regarded as a loveable freak. One reason is his physical makeup. Thin and tallish, he has a parenthesis-like stoop, spidery fingers, and a long, wry, gentle face governed by a generous, wandering nose. When he plays, this already striking facial arrangement, which is overlaid with an endless grille of wrinkles and furrows, becomes knotted into unbelievable grimaces of pain, as if the music were pulling unbearably tight an inner drawstring. (At rest or in motion, Russell has one of the classic physiognomies of the century; C. Aubrey Smith's and John L. Lewis' seem barely finished beside it.) The other reason is his style, which is often considered hopelessly eccentric because of its deceptive coating of squeaks, coppery tone, querulousness, growls, and overall hesitancy, which suggests that, if he played any note wrong, Russell feared he might irreparably damage it. An equally confusing fact about Russell is that for almost two decades he has been chiefly identified with innumerable Eddie Condon groups, which over the years have created a distinctly sallow and mechanical tradition, compounded mainly of the more adaptable facets of New Orleans jazz, Chicago jazz, and small-band swing. This association, though, has done more good than harm to Russell, for many of the men in these groups have been indifferent or mediocre musicians who, like the inepts so often surrounding Bix Beiderbecke (one of whom was actually named Rank), have, as unintentional reflectors for Russell, emphasized that he is one of the sanest and most original stylists in all jazz.

Russell can be devastating in a slow blues. Sidling softly into the lower register, where he gets a tone that is a cross between the low-thyroid murmurings of Joe Marsala and the bejowled utterances of Jimmy Noone, he will issue, after some preliminary blinking and squinting (as if he had just entered a bright room from a dark street), a series of crablike, irregularly staccato phrases, each shaken by a bone-worrying vibrato and each clamped tightly against its predecessor, lest any distractions leak in to cool off what he has in mind. After this, he may rocket up a couple of octaves and adopt a quavery, gnashing manner, or he may introduce dark, stuttering growls which seem to lacerate what he is playing so severely that one is invariably surprised that there is any sound at all left at the close of the solo. In faster tempos, Russell often assumes a jaunty, hat-over-the-ears manner, full of trills, sudden drops behind the beat (like an orator abruptly slowing down and underlining each word with a thump), nervous vaultings around the scale, and a gasping, old-womanish tone just this side of a shriek. Russell is also one of the great ensemble performers. One moment he will idle dispiritedly along in the middle register, as if he were trapped between the other horns and were looking for a way out, and the next, breaking free, he will rear back into a retarding, soaring wail that runs along the outermost edge of pitch—an area Russell frequently inhabits—forcing one to the edge of one's seat, until, with superb navigation, he lands unerringly on the note he began reaching for several measures before. At the end of a number, one realizes that, one way and another, Russell has managed to wrap it in a swirling, rococo cocoon that preserves its heat and glorifies its design.

Russell is in all of his myriad best forms in five recent releases. Three of them—"Portrait of Pee Wee" (Counterpoint), "Pee Wee Russell Plays Pee Wee" (Stere-o-craft), and "52nd Street Scene: Tony Scott and the All Stars" (Coral)—were made not along ago, and the rest—"Mild and Wild: Wild Bill Davison" and "Condon a la Carte" (Commodore)—are taken from a series of Commodore recordings set down in the early forties. Russell appears on sixteen of the twenty-four Commodores in half a dozen groups, which include such men as Max Kaminsky, Davison, Brad Gowans, George Brunis, Fats Waller, George Wettling, and Sid Catlett. Aside from the generally tattered, hurrying ensembles, there are often surprisingly eloquent solos, the best of them by Davison, Kaminsky, Gowans, Waller, and Russell, who moves from hoarse, snuffing low-register work, in "Panama" and "Save Your Sorrow," to excited gesticulations in the upper ranges in

"Ballin' the Jack" and "That's a Plenty," one of the most abandoned efforts of its kind ever made.

The Russell on the newer records is startlingly different. The frameworks are roughly those of small-band Kansas City jazz, and the materials include blues and standards and no Dixieland tunes. The Counterpoint has such men as Ruby Braff, Bud Freeman, Vic Dickenson, and Nat Pierce; the Stere-o-craft has only a rhythm section made up of Pierce, Steve Jordan, Walter Page, and George Wettling; and the Coral—an attempt to re-create some of the types of music that could be heard up to ten or twelve years ago on Fifty-second Street—has several groups, one of which is allotted two numbers and is made up of, among others, Russell, Scott, Joe Thomas, J. C. Higginbotham, Wilbur de Paris, Al Casey, and Denzil Best. Of the nineteen selections, the "Blues for 'the Street,'" on the Coral, is the best. A long, gossipy, marvelously relaxed blues, terminating in one of those remarkable loafing-in-the-sun ensembles invented in the late thirties by swing musicians, the piece reaches its climax after de Paris's statement, when Russell puts on his slippers, shuffles into the lower register, and produces, in his first chorus, a tight, bobbing, ruminative series of phrases—some so soft they are no more than tissues of breath—that have the discretion of an inner monologue and that are as affecting as anything he has recorded. Even in the standard tunes, he plays with a softness of tone and inflection that makes his Commodore work appear rather feverish, and although he displays his growl on the Stere-o-craft in "The Lady's in Love," it doesn't have the aching, emery quality it had fifteen years ago but seems only good-humored self-mimicry. Dickenson is the steadiest of his associates, and in "That Old Feeling," on the Counterpoint, plays a snorting, stamping solo, while throughout the record Freeman emits further variations on the solo he has been at work on for several decades. The rest of the accompaniment is adequate, except for the rhythm section of the Stere-o-craft, which is waterlogged from beginning to end. Russell's sails, however, are always filled.

February 21

ROACH, BLAKEY & P. J. JONES, INC.

ONE OF THE most remarkable things about Charlie Parker at the height of his powers was that he influenced almost every type of instrumentalist of malleable age, in an order that went roughly like this: pianists, other alto saxophonists, trumpeters, drummers, baritone saxophonists, tenor saxophonists, trombonists, and bassists. There were Charlie Parkers everywhere, all of them unavailingly attempting to convert their instruments into alto saxophones. Trumpeters, in particular, were notorious imitators; for a time, they abandoned all the rude, brassy properties of their instrument for a bland, rubbery, saxophonelike tone, which acted as a perfect cushion for the thousand and one Parker-inspired notes that constituted the average solo chorus. Although many alto saxophonists are still indistinguishable from Parker, most of the other instruments have, if permanently changed in other respects, begun to regain their original shapes. There is one startling exception—the drums. Led by Max Roach, who first worked with Parker at the age of seventeen and who at the same time was absorbing the work of such pre-Parker innovators as the drummers Jo Jones, Sid Catlett, and Kenny Clarke, the performers on these instruments have almost completed a revolution that represents possibly the broadest technical change ever to affect a jazz instrument. Roach, Art Blakey, and Philly Joe Jones (no relation to Jo Jones) have been the most headlong rebels (*their* most avid disciples include, among others, Elvin Jones, Art Taylor, Roy Haynes, and Louis Hayes), and three of their recent records—"Deeds, Not Words: Max Roach New Quintet" (Riverside), "Art Blakey's Jazz Messengers with Thelonious Monk" (Atlantic), and "Blues for Dracula: Philly Joe Jones Sextet" (Riverside)—provide ample and occasionally brilliant demonstrations of their various gospels. (There is another and quite different school of modern drummers, headed by such men as Shelly Manne, Joe Morello, Ed Shaughnessy, and Louis Bellson, who are, by and large, no less accomplished than Blakey, Roach, and Jones. But they fall between the great swing drummers and the avant-gardists. Though under the spell of Roach, Manne is fundamentally an extremely sensitive swing drummer, with overtones of Jo Jones and Dave Tough in his work; Morello, a crisp, crackling performer, owes much to Buddy Rich; Shaughnessy, an expert wire-brush performer, has listened to both Jo Jones and Roach; and Bellson, an extraordinary technician, resembles both Rich and Gene Krupa.)

The rebellion has gradually altered every piece of drum equipment. In the thirties, the average set of drums recalled a late-Victorian parlor. It included a large parade-size bass drum that emitted subterranean Robesonlike tones; a thick, sonorous snare drum; two or three tomtoms that were lesser versions of the bass drum; four or five cymbals, often hung from looped metal stands like those once used to support bird cages, and including the high-hat, a crash cymbal, a Chinese cymbal, and a couple of ride cymbals, mostly similar to the invincible Bismarckian cymbals used by nineteenth-century German brass bands;

a variety of bric-a-brac, consisting of tuned hollow gourds (called temple blocks), chimes, wood blocks, timpani, and at least one cowbell; and, finally, drumsticks that frequently approached billy clubs in size and heft. Modern drummers have whittled away about fifty pounds of that equipment. The bass drum has shrunk in some cases, to half its old size, and gives off a pinched, final sound. The snare drum, now the thickness of a frying pan, produces—partly because of its shallowness and partly because it is usually tightly snared and muffled—a flat, clapping sound, as of palm fronds in a strong breeze. There is generally one tomtom, again a diminutive version of the bass drum, while the cymbals, which are uniformly lighter, now number only the high-hat cymbals, a slightly heavier crash cymbal, and a thin, tremulous ride cymbal the size of a hoop. The drumsticks, more often than not, are elongated toothpicks. (For some reason, the Roach-Blakey-Jones division of modern drummers has just about given up wire brushes, which is too bad; in the hands of men like Jo Jones, Catlett, O'Neil Spencer and Tough, the brushes, with their subtle, needling delicacy, could be even more exhilarating than sticks.) The total effect, which is nearly the direct opposite of the earlier drum sets, is falsetto, chattery and nervous.

Indeed, an aggressive nervousness is the secret of the new drumming. While the older men, with all their equipment, filled a fairly unobtrusive supporting role, setting off ensembles and soloists with relaxed, comparatively simple highlights—rimshots, the swimming sound of the high-hat, the pad-pad of brushes—performers like Roach, Blakey, and Jones, with practically no equipment at all, have pushed themselves perfervidly and steadily into a queer, semi-independent position in the ensemble almost level with that of the melody instruments. (As a result, they are frequently and confusingly termed "melodic" drummers, which apparently means that they are melodic in that they use, like the great drummers of the past, a fairly wide degree of shading and timbre, or that they are melodic because they are attempting, through the use of overbearing, frequently uninterrupted rhythmic patterns, to raise the drum from the role of a supporting instrument to that of a melody instrument.) This invasion has been brought about by sheer force and by some radical technical departures. The modern drummer has shifted the basic marking of the beat from the bass drum, which he uses only for accents, to the ride cymbal and the high-hat, on the last of which he relentlessly sounds the afterbeat by metronomically clapping its cymbals shut with a choshing effect. Most important, this drummer worships the rhythmically oblique. Except when he is concerned with the ride cymbal and the high-hat, almost every motion the drummer makes, whether in the background or in solos, goes toward a collection of purposely disjointed out-of-metre patterns, which, carried to their farthest limits (Roach) result in a totally separate, arrhythmic wall of noise. As a result, three essentials of background jazz drumming—taste, variety, and control—have been practically lost sight of. Unlike the older drummers, who valued silence, dynamics, and the emphasizing coloring effects of using different parts of their set behind different instruments—sticks on a closed high-hat (the ticking of a large clock) behind a clarinet, wire brushes on cymbals (rustling silk) behind a piano, sticks on a ride cymbal (a cheerful belling sound) behind a trumpet—many modern drummers rely loudly and exclusively on the ride cymbal, an addiction that, after a time, creates an aggravating monotone that seems to drain all individual color out of the melodic instruments. In addition, many of these drummers have not yet mastered the complexities of out-of-rhythm playing, particularly in their solos, so the conflicting arrhythmic patterns they build tend simply to cancel each other out, leaving no rhythm at all.

Roach, unfortunately, is an excellent example. A first-rate technician, he has an intense, mosquitolike touch on his instrument. Yet the effect of his backing up is that of ten drummers playing at once. He fills in every chink with an unbroken succession of dum-de-da strokes, triplets, rolls, and staccato accents scattered, as if he were sowing seed, on every part of his set (he is, however, never far from the ride cymbal), and punctuated from time to time with bass-drum "bombs," which unlike true punctuation, are not pauses but only intensify the din. Consequently, when Roach takes a solo he is dismayingly like a non-stop talker who finally forces the group around him into silence while he rattles on and on. And, though perfectly executed, his solos are made up of so many contradicting rhythms and disconnected, rapidly rising and falling pyramids of sound that the beat, which they are supposed to be embroidering, disappears. Indeed, it is not unusual to find oneself hypnotized by the lightning concatenation of sounds in a Roach solo, and then, astonishingly, to discover that it has been managed wholly without imparting rhythm.

Blakey, five years older than Roach, who is thirty-four, has learned from both Roach and Catlett. He is a raucous, uneven, and sometimes primitive performer who gets a stuffy, closeted tone and who plays, now and then, with such nervous power that he is apt to drown the stoutest musician under florid, steaming cymbal work and jubilant, circuslike snare-drum rolls. Since he uses the Roach sort of embroidery only sparingly, the results can be devastating. After a spell of plain timekeeping, he will suddenly slip into a crooked, seemingly palsied series of staccato or double-time beats, snicked off on rims, cymbals, and drums, which introduce an irresistibly wild, impatient air. Blakey is an extremely dramatic, and occasionally melodramatic, soloist. He may begin a statement with a silence that is broken only by the sound of the high-hat on the afterbeat (which immediately creates a Chinese-water-torture tension), introduce some clicking sounds on the snare rims, abruptly spaced here and there with offbeats on the tomtom or snare, fall silent again, resume his knickety-knacking, this time hitting one stick against the other in the air, and then without warning launch into a fusillade of sounds between the snare and tomtom. He will then resort entirely to the snare, playing a hard, on-the-beat pattern, as if he were travelling very fast over a bumpy road, before departing on a second roundelay, which dissolves into staccato beats on the bass drum, executed with such rapidity that they blur into one prolonged beat, and climaxed by a crescendo snare-drum roll that calls the horns back from lunch. It is intense, perfectly spaced, declarative drumming that can, in its strongest moments, rattle one's jowls.

Jones, who is thirty-six, is, like any perfect revolutionist, both a violent development of the best of Roach and Blakey and a throwback to earlier methods. Obviously an admirer of Roach and Blakey, he is also an admitted student of Tough, Catlett and Rich. He achieves a neat, clipped sound, which also has much of the richer resilience of the swing drummers. When Jones is in balance—he sometimes inscrutably rolls all of Roach's and Blakey's sins into one enormous, deafening effusion—he is a master of silence, dynamics, and surprise. He will keep a steady, unobtrusive beat on the ride cymbal, repeatedly dotting it with flickering snare-drum accents, and, like Blakey, occasionally heighten it with double-time excursions, which, however, do not expunge the original beat but, instead, set up a fascinating undertow beneath the basic rhythm. (This tug-of-war technique is apt to baffle the soloist, who will grope confusedly from rhythm to rhythm, like a blind man.) Jones is becoming an increasingly formidable soloist. Close to Blakey and Catlett in this respect, he will open a medium-tempo solo with heavy, on-the-beat strokes that move inexorably back and forth, like ponderous seven-league strides, between the snare drum and the tomtom. Gradually, he will complicate this boom-boom-boom sequence by sliding in and out of double time and, after settling into full double time, with the listener running at top speed to keep up, he will abruptly fall back to the original beat, drop his volume, and begin soft, shuffling snare-drum rolls tamped down by a rhythmic pattern of rimshots that goes directly back to the work of Zutty Singleton. He will then rear up again and, like Catlett in his most inspired moments, rumble around his set, frequently bringing himself up short with explosive silences or hammering offbeat bass-drum thumps, which give one the impression of watching a fast uneven tennis match. Carrying this tension into the final ensemble, he will dart in and out of the holes in the melody with quick cymbal splashes (Tough) and fast, rounded double-time effects, as if he were a mongoose piling into a cobra, and then close with a giant, simmering cymbal stroke.

The LPs mentioned above are striking evidence of the power of Roach, Blakey, and Jones, for, with the exception of the one in which Monk appears, the records would be worthless without their leaders. In fact, Roach's record (with him are trumpet, tenor saxophone, tuba, and bass) is chiefly interesting for an unaccompanied medium-tempo drum solo (there are six other numbers) called "Conversation," which displays perfectly all of Roach's tendencies toward intricate, overlapping, rhythmless crosscurrents of sound that are, nonetheless, absorbing simply because they are carried out, in the manner of Art Tatum's piano playing, with such precision and authority. "Art Blakey's Jazz Messengers with Thelonious Monk," on the other hand, is a superb rhythmic exercise from start to finish, largely because of the unique combination of Monk and Blakey. (Also on hand for the six numbers—five of them Monk's—are trumpet, tenor saxophone, and bass.) Monk has his own devious, irrepressible, built-in rhythm section, and Blakey is the only drummer around who knows how to supplement it without getting in its way. The result is the very best a rhythm section can do; all the soloists sound twice as good as they really are. Blakey is a wonder behind Monk. On "In Walked Bud" a medium-tempo number, Monk begins with irregular, offbeat chords (Blakey counters with a long string of seemingly irrelevant tappings, as if he were a mason tunking bricks into place); Monk continues with expanded variations on the same figures (Blakey dodges lightly back and forth between the snare and tomtom, planting quick, skidding sounds); Monk loafs (Blakey loafs and then starts knocking his sticks against each other, as though baiting Monk); Monk, baited, resumes (Blakey joins him and closes the chorus with a swooshing roll that picks Monk up and drops him neatly into his second chorus). Jones' record would collapse without him. Working, in its five numbers, with cornet, trombone, tenor saxophone, piano, and bass, all of them rather diffuse performers, he employs every supporting mechanism in the book, including hushed, quick-breathing double-time figures on the high-hat at the start of the piano solo in "Blues for Dracula," pushing, ramshackle snare and tomtom work behind the tenor saxophone in "Ow!," and, at the end of the same number, some stunning ensemble accompaniment that recalls the best of Tough and Catlett. His solos, particularly a long one in "Ow!," are careful, remarkably graduated structures, full of surprises, varied timbres and good old-fashioned emotion. Jones, practically single-handed, is winding up the insurrection.

April 11

INDEX

INDEX